OECD Reviews on Local Job Creation

Engaging Employers and Developing Skills at the Local Level in Australia

OECD

BETTER POLICIES FOR BETTER LIVES

This document, as well as any data and any map included herein, are without prejudice to the status of or sovereignty over any territory, to the delimitation of international frontiers and boundaries and to the name of any territory, city or area.

Please cite this publication as:
OECD (2019), *Engaging Employers and Developing Skills at the Local Level in Australia*, OECD Reviews on Local Job Creation, OECD Publishing, Paris.
https://doi.org/10.1787/9789264304888-en

ISBN 978-92-64-30487-1 (print)
ISBN 978-92-64-30488-8 (pdf)

OECD Reviews on Local Job Creation
ISSN 2311-2328 (print)
ISSN 2311-2336 (online)

The statistical data for Israel are supplied by and under the responsibility of the relevant Israeli authorities. The use of such data by the OECD is without prejudice to the status of the Golan Heights, East Jerusalem and Israeli settlements in the West Bank under the terms of international law.

Photo credits: Cover © Pykha/Thinkstock by Getty Image/Fotolia

Corrigenda to OECD publications may be found on line at: *www.oecd.org/about/publishing/corrigenda.htm*.

Foreword

Australia has a healthy labour market, and this applies to the young people as well. The overall unemployment rate was 5.6% in 2017, which was below the OECD average of 5.8%. The share of youth (aged 20-24 years) not in employment, education, or training (NEETs) stood around 12% in 2017, which compares favourably to the OECD average of 15%. At the same time, globalisation, automation, and digitalisation are changing labour market demands, as well as the skills required of people entering employment. As the Australian job market evolves, it will be critical to ensure that the education system is well-connected to industry to facilitate smooth transitions from school to work.

This report sheds light on a number of key lessons and policy principles for better engaging Australian employers in skills development opportunities at the local level. Within the vocational education and training system, apprenticeship programmes mix on the job training with classroom-based learning. Expanding the availability and take-up of quality apprenticeship programmes and other work-based training opportunities can provide employers with a skilled workforce that is more agile in a rapidly evolving global economy. It can also support the creation of new employment opportunities for disadvantaged groups and contribute to Australia's regional economic development objectives by building the competitiveness of local growth sectors.

Broadening access and participation to apprenticeship programmes requires close collaboration and co-ordination at the local level between government, businesses, training providers, and workers. Case studies from New South Wales, Tasmania, and Queensland presented in this report illustrate the role that local leaders can play in shaping the education and training system to better respond to key growth sectors of the economy. They also show how apprenticeship programmes can better link disadvantaged groups, such as youth and Indigenous people, to good quality jobs.

This report is part of the Programme of Work of the OECD Local Economic and Employment Development (LEED) Programme. Created in 1982, the LEED Programme aims to contribute to the creation of more and better jobs in more productive and inclusive economies. It produces guidance to make the implementation of national policies more effective at the local level, while stimulating innovative practices on the ground. The OECD LEED Directing Committee, which gathers governments of OECD member and non-member countries, oversees the work of the LEED Programme. The main findings of the report were discussed at the 74th session of the OECD LEED Directing Committee on 15-16 November 2018. The final report was approved by Delegates at this session: CFE-LEED (2018)13.

Acknowledgements

This report has been prepared by the Centre for Entrepreneurship, SMEs, Regions and Cities (CFE), led by Lamia Kamal-Chaoui, Director. This work was conducted as part of the OECD's Local Economic and Employment Development (LEED) Programme in co-operation with the Australian Department of Education and Training.

This project on engaging local employers in skills development in Australia was co-ordinated by Jonathan Barr, Head of the Employment and Skills Unit within the Local Employment, Skills and Social Innovation (LESI) Division of CFE, under the supervision of Karen Maguire, Acting Head of LESI Division.

The principal authors of this report are Anna Choi (Policy Analyst) and Jonathan Barr (Head of Unit) from OECD/CFE. Sections of the report were drafted by a team of researchers at Miles Morgan Australia (Barbara Macnish, Naysa Brasil Teodoro and Catherine Manley). Beatriz Jambrina (Statistician) and Alessandro Kandiah (Policy Analyst) from the OECD/CFE also contributed to the development of this publication through statistical analysis and drafting support. Janine Treves (Digital Managing Editor, Public Affairs and Communications Directorate) provided editorial assistance and Pilar Philip (Publications and Event Co-ordinator, CFE) co-ordinated the publication process.

A number of OECD colleagues provided valuable input and feedback on the development of this report, including Anthony Mann (Head of Unit) from the Directorate of Education and Skills, and Katherine Mullock (Policy Analyst) from the Directorate of Employment, Labour and Social Affairs.

The OECD would like to thank colleagues within the Australia Department of Education and Training, including Fran Wylie, Anthony Krieg, and Andrej Pavkovic, who were instrumental in co-ordinating this project and providing valuable comments on the report.

Special thanks should also be given to local stakeholders in each of the case study areas that participated in meetings and provided documentation and comments that were critical to the production of the report. In particular, the OECD is grateful to Sydney Metro in New South Wales; STEMship in New South Wales; Dream, Believe, Achieve in Queensland; and Collective Ed in Tasmania.

Table of contents

Tables

Figures

Reader's Guide

This publication presents an analysis of key labour market and skills trends in Australia followed by examples of local programmes that are working closely with employers to align skills training to labour market demand.

Chapter 1 provides an overview of the current economic context in Australia, while Chapter 2 looks at national and regional key trends in vocational education and apprenticeship participation. Chapter 3 highlights results from the OECD survey of Australian employers, carried out from October – December 2017. To this end, the OECD worked in partnership with the Department of Education and Training to identify a suitable sample from the Australia Business Register database. This survey collected information from over 400 employers across Australia – 95% of the employers responding were small and medium-sized businesses with less than 250 employees.

Chapters 4-7 provide information on four case studies that were carried out at the local level to identify strengths and weaknesses in the implementation framework of skills policies in Australia. The case study areas were selected in consultation with the Department of Education and Training, with a view to identify initial lessons from a recent initiative to improve collaboration with local industry representatives in metropolitan areas. For each case study, interviews were undertaken with stakeholders in the fields of vocational training, employment, and economic development in order to collect evidence around local actions being taken to boost participation in apprenticeship and other work-based training programmes.

Acronyms and Abbreviations

ACT	Australian Capital Territory
AQF	Australian Qualifications Framework
COAG	Council of Australian Governments
GTO	Group Training Organisation
LEED	Local Economic and Employment Development
NEET	Not in Employment, Education or Training
NGO	Non-Governmental Organisation
NT	Northern Territory
NSW	New South Wales
OECD	Organisation for Economic Co-operation and Development
PIAAC	Programme for the International Assessment of Adult Competencies
PISA	Programme for International Student Assessment
QLD	Queensland
RDA	Regional Development Australia (RDA Hunter)
RTO	Registered Training Organisations
SA	Southern Australia
SES	Socio-Economic Status
SME	Small and Medium-sized Enterprise
STEM	Science, Technology, Engineering and Mathematics
TAFE	Technical and Further Education
TAS	Tasmania
VET	Vocational Education and Training
WA	Western Australia

Executive Summary

Apprenticeship programmes play a central role in ensuring that the supply of skills meets demand through their combination of both school-based learning and practical on the job training. In recent years, there has been a decline in the take-up of apprenticeships in Australia, with registrations more than halving from 376 800 in 2010-11 to 164 000 in 2016-17. The Australian Government has committed to working closer with industry through the Skilling Australians Fund with the goal of creating thousands of additional apprenticeships and traineeships.

The government can secure these outcomes by giving employers a stronger leadership role in steering training design and delivery. Responses to a 2017 OECD survey of Australian employers show that 50% of employers retain at least 75% of their apprentices on payroll when apprenticeship training is completed. Retention rates tend to be higher among SMEs, demonstrating the potential value of apprenticeship training for these firms. The lack of time and resources was the most common reported barrier to participation. A commonly cited concern about current programme delivery is poor collaboration with training organisations, inadequate off-the-job training and high dropout rates. However, over 75% of surveyed employers reported that they are interested in establishing stronger partnerships with local training providers going forward.

The following in-depth case studies were carried out to analyse in greater detail local examples of employer engagement:

- **Sydney Metro** is the biggest rail project in Australia and demonstrates the importance of co-ordination among relevant stakeholders to create customised solutions to skills and workforce development challenges within a local labour market.
- **STEMship** is a pre-employment programme based in Newcastle, New South Wales. It demonstrates how partnerships between the business and education sector can deliver skills training within emerging sectors of the local economy that are less vulnerable to automation.
- **Cowboys: Dream, Believe, Achieve Programme**, based in Queensland, is an example of a community organisation's leadership to deliver individually tailored training programmes to disadvantaged youth in the service sector.
- **Collective Education in Tasmania** is a pilot programme that aims to improve Year 12 completion rates by encouraging schools to work more closely with industry to ensure students gain practical and job-relevant skills. The programme also encourages networking between teachers, industry representatives and students.

These case studies illustrate the important role that local leaders can play in promoting apprenticeship participation. Local leadership from a regional development organisation, training provider, or community organisation can be especially effective in convincing employers to participate in an apprenticeship. Local infrastructure investments in roads, bridges, and public transport can also be used to provide incentives for new investments in apprenticeship training. Public policy can further support these efforts by setting social procurement targets that require a binding commitment from employers on offering quality apprenticeship opportunities. Finally, apprenticeship programmes can also be a useful training platform to target skills training to disadvantaged people.

The following recommendations for national and state governments in Australia emerge based on the analysis carried out in this report:

Local leadership matters

- **Strengthen local networks to generate stronger apprenticeship outcomes:** The national government in Australia could appoint local co-ordinators within regions that would focus on generating more collaboration around apprenticeships.
- **Encourage technical and further education (TAFE) institutions to conduct more outreach with employers and industry experts:** Ensure accountability frameworks for TAFEs take into account how often and intensely they engage with industry in the design and delivery of apprenticeship programmes.
- **Look at opportunities for City Deals to enable policy innovation within the apprenticeship system:** National and state governments can provide autonomy to cities and regions to manage skills training programmes with the goal of improving co-ordination and outreach to employers.

A flexible and customised training system can foster more participation

- **Ensure multidisciplinary pathways and flexible training arrangements within the Australia VET system:** To ensure that individuals develop both good generic skills alongside specific occupational competencies, national and state governments should encourage TAFEs and other training providers to combine competency units and training packages.
- **Provide targeted support to SMEs to participate in apprenticeships:** National and state governments should work closer with professional associations to market apprenticeships to SMEs, who tend to retain their apprentices.
- **Align training with the demands of emerging and growing industries:** Regional development organisations should aim to design apprenticeship programmes in STEM-related occupations, which are often a critical source of new job creation at the local level.

Targeting disadvantaged groups can improve labour market participation

- **Recognise the importance of mentoring within apprentices to complete their training:** National and state governments can encourage a mentorship component within apprenticeship delivery, especially for at-risk youth and Aboriginal Torres and Strait Islanders.
- **Consider setting social procurement targets to have a binding commitment from employers on apprenticeship training:** National and state governments should steer employers to invest in more skills training, especially for disadvantaged groups, by attaching specific apprenticeship requirements to procurement bids.

Assessment and Recommendations

Providing equal opportunities for individuals and workers to gain the skills demanded in the local economy is critical to create a vibrant labour market. At a macro level, Australia's economy performs well and has an unemployment rate below the OECD average. But there are challenges to sustain economic performance over the long term. Notably, there has been a decline in apprenticeship participation since 2012. The total number of apprenticeship commencements in the financial year 2011-12 were 376 800 while they dropped to around 162 600 in 2016-17. Several regional economies in Australia are undergoing significant structural adjustment. This downward trend is most prominent in the states of New South Wales, Victoria, South Australia, and Queensland.

Many factors can affect and shape why employers and individuals participate in skills development and apprenticeship programmes. Going forward, the Australian government should consider the following recommendations with regard to improving the engagement of local employers in skills development opportunities:

The Skilling Australians Fund can secure better employment outcomes provided that employers take a leadership role in steering design and delivery

The Skilling Australians Fund is a recent commitment by the government to help more Australians acquire the skills they need through apprenticeships, traineeships and employment-related training opportunities. From 2017-22, approximately AUD 1.5 billion will be available from the government, combined with matching funding from the state and territory governments with the goal of creating thousands of additional apprenticeships, traineeships and employment-related training opportunities.

This joint effort with the state and territory governments is an excellent opportunity to strengthen the design and delivery of apprenticeship programmes, ensuring that they are fit for purpose to meet employer demand at the local level, while also stimulating productivity improvements across all regions of Australia. By placing a strong emphasis on accountability, transparency, and clear outcomes, this programme can ensure that resources are allocated efficiently to boost apprenticeship participation in occupations across industries of future growth and that face skill shortages at the state and territory level.

Employers will play a critical role in driving more participation in apprenticeship and work-based learning opportunities. The government should examine how best to ensure programmes provide the right incentives for employers to participate in the vocational education and training system. It is important to foster and encourage business-education partnerships to ensure that the supply of skills meets industry demands.

Strengthen local leadership networks to generate stronger apprenticeship outcomes

In-depth fieldwork undertaken for this study has identified the importance of having a coherent and close network of local stakeholders including government, industry/employers and training sectors involved in the implementation of apprenticeship policies. This is essential to ensure that the design and delivery of programmes responds to different local needs and demands, while also improving communication among relevant parties to provide the necessary support to employers. As implementation of the Skilling Australians Fund goes ahead, state and territory governments should examine opportunities to stimulate collaboration at the local level, which will be a critical success factor in fostering apprenticeship participation for both individuals and employers. Appointing or delegating a local co-ordinator can help ensure that collaboration delivers real results on the ground.

For example, as part of the Sydney Metro project, the Skills and Employment Advisory Group (SEAG) was created which includes different government agencies (both state and national level) as well as industry partners with a shared interest in Sydney's workforce development objectives. This type of partnership facilitates knowledge and information sharing relevant to training and as well as examining solutions to address skills shortages within local industries. The SEAG members had decision-making powers, met regularly and came from a cross-section of different organisations such as TAFE NSW, NSW Department of Industry, Australian Government Department of Education and Training, Sydney Metro contractors, and Training Services NSW. Sydney Metro led the work of co-ordinating the group to convince the involved stakeholders to recognise the value of having a shared approach and working together towards that goal.

In North Queensland, the Cowboys rugby league club initiated the Dream, Believe, and Achieve (DBA) programme to increase youth engagement in the labour market. This programme also emphasised local community and business networks to generate partnerships with training providers to deliver individually tailored VET programmes in the hospitality sector for Aboriginal and Torres Strait Islander youth.

Similarly, the Tasmanian government emphasised partnerships and worked on a new system called Collective Ed, together with the Paul Ramsay Foundation, that focuses on collaborative design and adaptive leadership in educational programmes. As suggested by the name, at its core, Collective Ed adopted a new approach to gain collective understanding of the challenges and achieve common goals by bringing together students, teachers, parents, schools, communities and business and industry leaders.

Building and forming formal local governance networks can be challenging. It requires co-ordination, governance structures and leadership within the community. A common theme that emerged from the case studies was the difficulty of convincing employers of the value of working with government to co-design training programmes. In these cases, having strong leadership from the government as well as a formal co-ordinating organisation is critical to leverage existing local networks of employers. For example, Sydney Metro took the co-ordination lead and had strong leadership from Transport for NSW, the state government department in charge of transport services in New South Wales. The creation of SEAG recognised the need for a close formal industry-government-training partnership.

Another common success factor relates to a long-term commitment to build collaboration among different stakeholders. It takes time to convince different parties about the importance of working together so that the training provided to students improves their chances of finding a job. For the STEMship project, RDA Hunter took on the co-ordinating role, had extensive consultation sessions with local industry, and worked with Hunter TAFE (the partner RTO) for delivery. RDA Hunter has been engaging with businesses, schools, universities, government agencies and community leaders since 2009 through STEM education and workforce development programs. With this active engagement and track record of successful delivery of different programmes in schools, RDA Hunter was able to gain respect and trust in the local community.

Encourage vocational education and training providers to conduct more outreach with local employers and industry experts

Another important factor for success will be ensuring that vocational education and training providers do active outreach with local employers. This is crucial to ensure that curriculum development as well as training delivery are tested and informed by local industry. Results from the OECD survey of employers suggest that collaboration between employers and training providers needs to be strengthened. This is primarily because local employers and industry experts are seldom involved in defining the current training packages. Consequently, survey respondents felt that this can lead to programmes that are not necessarily relevant and/or have students leave pre-apprenticeship programmes without relevant experience and knowledge.

Creating these types of partnerships may involve the creation of local employer networks, which directly engage TAFEs in training design and curriculum development. In some cases, it might be best to engage more directly with professional associations or sector bodies that represent a group of employers. This is particularly the case for small and medium-sized employers who face unique barriers to engagement.

Looking at lessons from the case studies, STEMship focused on building a close relationship with industry and engaging local employers through RDA Hunter in order to design and structure more customised training activities. With the local economy shifting towards knowledge-intensive sectors that traditionally do not engage much with the VET sector, it was essential to actively engage employers in the design of the programme. By involving industry partners and consulting employers in STEM-related fields to drive curriculum development, the STEMship project was able to identify the necessary skills and align the training design with local industry demands. Despite the small number of students (in absolute terms) who participated in the programme from its beginning, in 2017, 100% of the participants went on to continue an apprenticeship or other VET programmes upon completion.

Different parts of the Sydney Metro project had close partnerships with local employers. The Sydney Metro Upskilling Programme has contractor-led training to ensure the training meets both business and individuals' training needs. Another flagship programme of the Sydney Metro project is the Infrastructure Skills Centres, which focuses on providing up-to-date infrastructure for skills training and addressing the skills requirements of jobs across major construction projects in the region. Infrastructure Skills Centres work in conjunction with TAFE NSW and provide industry-led and co-designed training curriculum that is responsive to the needs of the local economy.

Look at opportunities for City Deals to enable policy innovation within the skills training and apprenticeship system

City Deals in Australia aim to bring together different levels of government alongside community organisations and the private sector to build long-term partnerships at the local level. Given the diversity and characteristics of the cities across Australia, City Deals acknowledge the importance of tailoring the approach from design to delivery and implementation. The Australian Government has highlighted six general themes for City Deals: infrastructure and investment; livability and sustainability; housing; innovation and digital opportunities; governance, city, planning and regulation; and jobs and skills. The Western Sydney City Deal also delivers on the Greater Sydney Commission's Western City District Plan, which involves collaboration with the eight local government authorities in the Western Sydney region to co-ordinate land use and development over the next 20 to 40 years.

Western Sydney was one of the first three City Deals implemented in Australia and includes several good elements for building public-private partnerships within the community. The skills and education elements of the Western Sydney City Deal are strongly linked to the City Deal's major infrastructure projects, including the construction of the new Western Sydney Airport and surrounding Aerotropolis precinct at Badgerys Creek. One of the key features of the Aerotropolis will be an integrated education facility, the Aerospace Institute, which will focus on education and skills training opportunities for emerging industries in the local area. This new Institute will include a high-performance secondary school, a VET facility and a STEM university that focus on the region's growth industries such as aviation and construction. Also, TAFE NSW will work with the Australian Government and Western Sydney Airport (WSA) Co to create a Skills Exchange near the future Western Sydney Airport to provide local skills training to develop the workforce needed to construct the Airport and other major projects.

Evidently creating such new facilities involves extensive planning and resources in addition to close public-private partnerships. The Aerospace Institute will be made possible through public-private partnership and co-investment from the government and industry. As an effort to engage three layers of government effectively, the Western Sydney City Deal includes a long-term governance arrangement as well as an agreed implementation plan. In order to increase funding and investment opportunities, the NSW Government is establishing the Western Sydney Investment Attraction Office to draw interests for both domestic and international investment.

Australia can look to other OECD countries for important lessons regarding the implementation of City Deals and their potential role in fostering more participation in skills training at the local level. In the United Kingdom, City Deals have provided regions with more autonomy to develop skills training approaches in partnership with employers. For example, in both Manchester and Leeds, City Deals have led to the establishment of local apprenticeship hubs, which aim to provide a "one-stop" shop service model to employers, with the goal of ensuring a co-ordinated outreach approach to employers (especially SMEs) among public agencies. Both of these UK cities have been successful in promoting and encouraging increased apprenticeship participation within their communities.

Ensure multidisciplinary pathways and flexible training arrangements within the VET system

Flexibility within apprenticeships programmes and having a multidisciplinary training model in VET curriculum proved to be essential for success across the case studies examined for this report. The Sydney Metro Apprenticeship programme, a flagship programme under the Sydney Metro project, was developed so that apprentices are hired by a Group Training Organisation (GTO) rather than a specific contractor to allow rotation of apprentices among companies when required. GTOs play a key role in the apprenticeship system by employing 8.5% of Australian apprentices and trainees as at end of 2017. This arrangement has allowed apprentices to complete their apprenticeship training within a network of companies as opposed to a single employer. This type of flexible design can enable both employers and apprentices to find a better match and more opportunities, particularly for apprentices to have exposure to different types of training, skills and industries.

The STEMship project also had a multidisciplinary learning framework with 19 competency units and 7 different training packages including computer assisted design, electronics, mathematics, basic engineering, and workplace skills. Most of the learning is done on a project and modular basis, where students work in teams and learn modules of different units of competency in a single project.

In order to scale up these cases, aligning the traditional VET funding and delivery models with a multidisciplinary model is essential in Australia. Currently, VET funding policy tends to favour more specific qualifications. However, while VET qualifications comprise core units of competency from a specific training package, a large number of VET qualifications offer a range of elective options, often enabling students to add units of competency from other training packages to their qualification. At the higher education level, funding for multidisciplinary training exists, where students can graduate with a substantive share of elective units. Policy makers should consider how to further strengthen the offer of multidisciplinary training options within the VET sector. In this context, the Australian Industry and Skills Committee (AISC) is working towards the development of cross-sector units of competency across range of areas that could support a multidisciplinary model. Areas where this work is being developed include: automation, big data, digital skills, cybersecurity, supply chains, environmental sustainability, work and participation, inclusion of people with a disability, consumer engagement through social media.

Finally, it should be noted that a multidisciplinary approach could also pose some financial as well as administrative challenges to RTOs. Delivering multiple training packages at once means drawing on more resources (e.g. trainers and equipment) per student than what is required by traditional VET courses in Australia. During the two years of STEMship delivery, TAFE NSW has been able to restructure resources, schedules and systems in an effective way, but other RTOs might find this process challenging in terms of resource allocation.

Recognise the importance of mentoring and support for apprentices to complete their training

Having supportive mentors who have had similar apprenticeship experience or those from the same industry is critical for apprentices, particularly for those coming from a disadvantaged background. One of the main concerns that Australian employers expressed in the OECD survey regarding apprenticeship participation was issues related to the retention of apprentices. Mentoring can be effective in identifying the concerns of apprentices and tracking their progress and satisfaction throughout their training, which in turn can lower the likelihood of attrition. Thus, putting more importance on mentoring can be beneficial for both the employers and apprentices. Programmes such as the Industry Specialist Mentoring for Australian Apprenticeships (ISMAA) go in the right direction of providing assistance to apprentices and trainees who are experiencing barriers to completing their training.

All of the case studies emphasised strong mentoring support as one of the success factors of the projects. The Dream, Believe, Achieve Programme (DBA) is an excellent example which incorporates mentoring in its delivery. Mentors actively work with apprentices to identify goals and barriers to participating in training programs. Both STEMship and Sydney Metro Apprentices Programme also had mentoring support for students throughout the programme.

Consider setting social procurement targets to have a binding commitment from employers on skills training

Another lesson learned from the case studies is the possibility of integrating training and employment requirements within the public tendering process. This can sometimes be challenging as it can cause administrative delays in issuing and finalising a contract. One approach taken by Sydney Metro is to require tenderers to include their approach to contribute towards Sydney Metro's workforce development goals in any proposals. Although the results are yet to be measured, this has been successful so far because the bidders compete based on finding innovative approaches to meet Sydney's workforce development objectives. It is also important to ensure that contractual targets have broad minimum requirements for the whole project with specific and tailored targets for each contract package (based on the type of contractor and project delivery phase). Lessons from other OECD countries highlight the important role social procurement targets can play in fostering inclusion at the local level. In Switzerland, cantons (states) often include social responsibility measures within their procurement targets to promote apprenticeship and skills training, especially among disadvantaged groups. In the Czech Republic, a best practice manual on setting social procurement targets has been developed by the Ministry of Labour and shared with local municipalities.

Provide more customised and targeted support to SMEs to offer apprenticeship opportunities

Finding and training apprentices can be a challenging task for employers, particularly those without support or administrative capacity. Not surprisingly, the OECD survey found that the most commonly cited barrier to apprenticeships among employers was the lack of resources and support for training apprentices, which can be a time-consuming and resource-heavy process. This was commonly reported by small-sized firms regardless of the sector. Nearly 90% of the large firms with 100 to 249 employees that participated in the OECD survey provide apprenticeships, whereas less than a quarter of firms with less than 10 employees report that they offer apprenticeship opportunities. However, it should be noted that the results from the OECD survey cannot be generalised, and that the Australian Government provides support for employers and apprentices through the Australian Apprenticeships Incentives Program (AAIP), the Australian Apprenticeship Support Network (AASN), and Trade Support Loans (TSL) programmes.

A larger share of micro-sized firms indicate that they usually retain their apprentices than larger firms. For instance, 50% of employers with 2-9 employees reported they keep all of their apprentices, while about 12% of employers with 250 or more employees reported retaining all of their apprentices. This may suggest that the demand and intention to retain apprentices may be higher among micro and small firms relative to larger employers in Australia.

It can be challenging for small and medium-sized firms to have sufficient capacity and resources to participate in apprenticeship programmes. While this may not be the sole reason for not providing apprenticeship opportunities, policy makers should consider ways to better channel resources and support to SMEs to hire and train apprentices. Given that the retention rate of apprentices is higher among small-sized employers than large firms, it is even more important to provide support for SMEs that seek apprentices to maintain or improve the future skills levels of the organisation and to improve productivity.

Smaller employers can benefit greatly from apprentices. Governments and social partners can support smaller employers by encouraging employers to find ways to share the responsibility and risks associated with the provision of apprenticeships; promoting bodies that work with groups of small employers to co-ordinate training; supporting small employers with the administration and provision of apprenticeships.

Align training offers and delivery with the demands of emerging and growing industries

The OECD survey of Australian employers showed that a frequently cited reason for not offering apprenticeships related to inadequate off-the-job training that is not relevant to the company's needs. Most of the Australian employers in the OECD survey agreed that they value apprentices with advanced numeracy and literacy skills. Training organisations need to ensure they deliver programmes that provide apprentices with relevant skills, including digital skills, for emerging industries in the local economy.

The Western Sydney City Deal focuses on aligning skills development programmes (across schools, VET, and higher education) to the industries that are growing in the local economy, such as construction, aerospace and aviation. This involves building a new Aerotropolis precinct to act as a hub drawing relevant industries together and generating synergies between them. In order to provide relevant and high quality training and to ensure access to these training opportunities, the NSW government plans to establish a permanent VET facility focusing on these emerging industries. Furthermore, in line with the VET facility and the connection to the aerospace and aviation industries, the NSW government will build a new public high school focusing on STEM and other relevant skills needed for future jobs in the local area.

Chapter 1. Recent labour market and skills trends at the regional level in Australia

This chapter provides an overview of recent labour market and skills trends in Australia. The Australian economy has experienced steady growth in overall productivity levels over the past ten years. The unemployment rate is lower than the OECD average. With a low unemployment rate, about 34% of Australian employers find it challenging to fill in vacancies, particularly for skilled trade positions. A similar pattern holds true for skill shortages across all states and territories. According to the Internet Vacancy Index, over the past five years, job advertisements have increased by 31% nationally (in trend terms).

Recent economic trends

The Australian economy experienced considerable growth in the last decade. As shown in Figure 1.1, gross domestic product (GDP) per capita levels have been steadily growing in Australia since the early 1990s. This growth rate in Australia is higher than the OECD average. In part, this solid growth is attributable to high commodity prices, prompt fiscal policy responses, and a resilient financial system (OECD, 2017[1]).

Figure 1.1. GDP per capita, Australia and the OECD average, 1990-2017

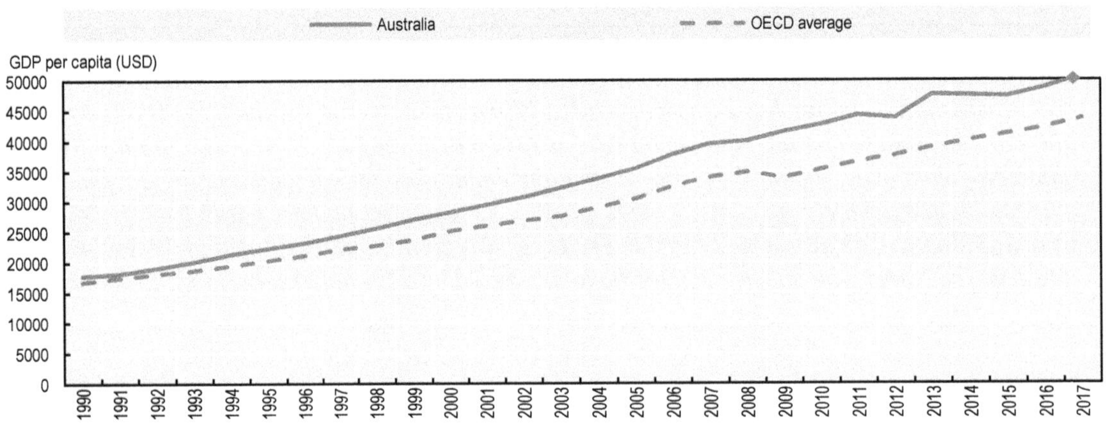

Note: GDP per capita data are measured in US dollars at current prices and PPPs.
Source: OECD (2018), Gross domestic product (GDP) (indicator). doi: 10.1787/dc2f7aec-en.

StatLink https://doi.org/10.1787/888933931656

Even though GDP per capita has been growing, Australia along with other developed countries faces the risk of a low growth trap. As reported in the most recent OECD economic survey, productivity growth in Australia has decelerated since the peak in the late 1990s similar to other OECD countries, but remains in line with the long term average (OECD, 2017[1]) (Figure 1.2).

Figure 1.2. Labour productivity growth[1] (per hour worked) has slowed in Australia

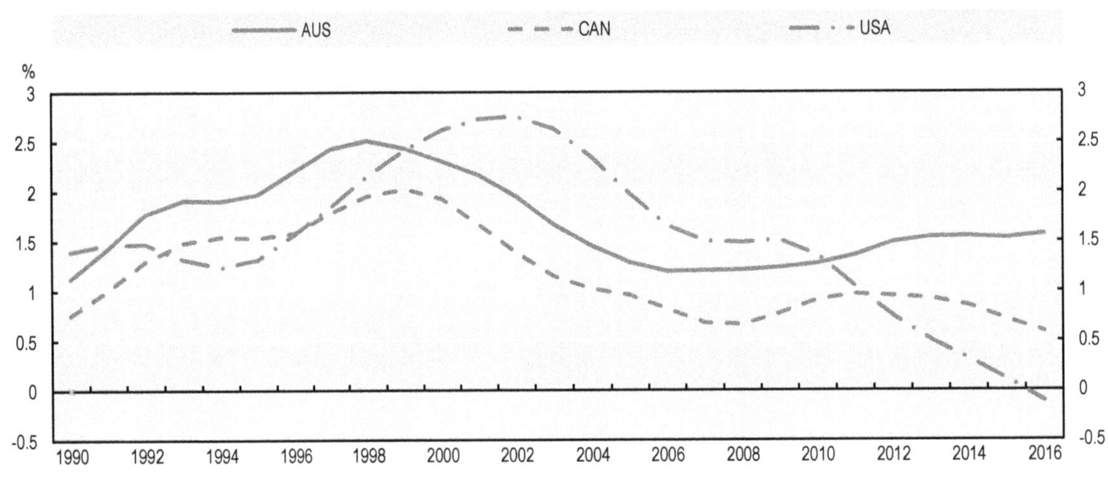

Note: 1. Data smoothed by the Hodrick-Prescott filter
Source: The Conference Board (2016), The Conference Board Total Economy Database, May 2016. OECD, 2017.

StatLink https://doi.org/10.1787/888933931675

Labour market trends

Unemployment rates

During the last two decades, Australia has had a relatively low unemployment rate compared to the OECD average even during the recent Global Financial Crisis (GFC). The seasonally adjusted unemployment rate among the working age population in Australia has been declining since 1999 except for the peak during the crisis. Also, a broad upward trend was recorded between 2011 and 2014, linked to the end of the mining boom, before trending downwards since 2015. In the last few years, the average unemployment rate has decreased to about 5.6% in Australia (see Figure 1.3), with women having a slightly higher unemployment rate than men (Figure 1.4).

Figure 1.3. Unemployment rate, Australia and the OECD, 1999-2017

Harmonised unemployment rate (%)

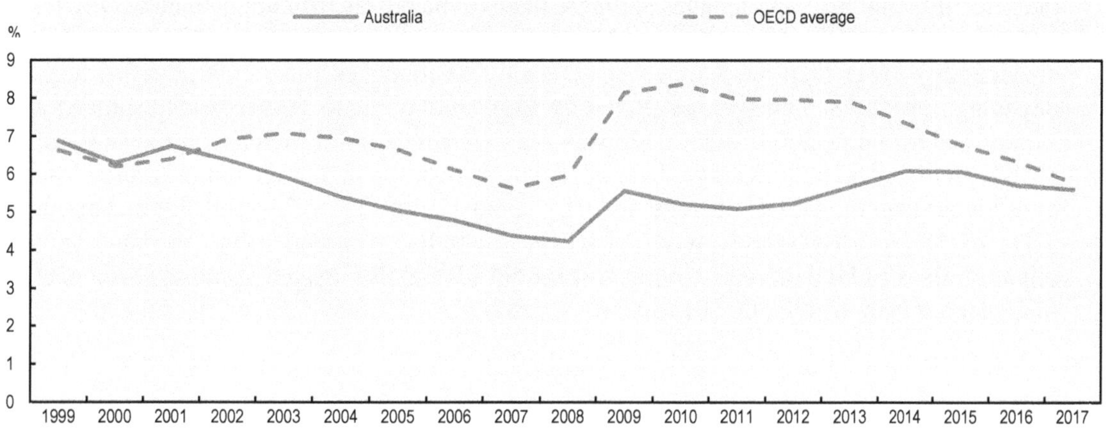

Note: Harmonised unemployment rates define the unemployed as people of working age who are without work, are available for work, and have taken specific steps to find work. The uniform application of this definition results in estimates of unemployment rates that are more internationally comparable than estimates based on national definitions of unemployment. This indicator is measured in numbers of unemployed people as a percentage of the labour force and it is seasonally adjusted. The labour force is defined as the total number of unemployed people plus those in civilian employment.
Source: OECD (2018), Harmonised unemployment rate (HUR) (indicator). doi: 10.1787/52570002-en.

StatLink https://doi.org/10.1787/888933931694

Figure 1.4. Unemployment rates by gender in Australia (2000-17)

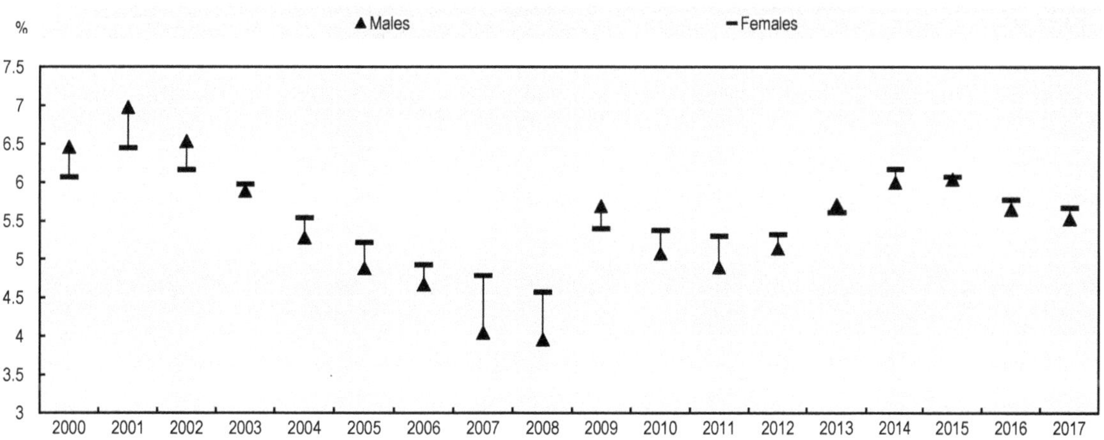

Source: OECD (2018), Unemployment rate (indicator). doi: 10.1787/997c8750-en.

StatLink https://doi.org/10.1787/888933931713

Labour market conditions for youth (15-24 year olds) in Australia deteriorated at the onset of the GFC and continued to weaken in the following years until 2017. The youth unemployment rate increased substantially up from 8.7% in September 2008 to a post-GFC high of 14.4% in October 2014. Youth labour market conditions have improved since 2017, reflecting the particularly strong pace of employment growth more generally over the period. However, youth unemployment still remains above the levels recorded at the onset of the GFC in September 2008 and, despite having declined to 11.6% in May 2018, it remains more than double the rate for all persons (aged 15 years and over). While it is encouraging that more people are participating in full-time education (52.9% in May 2018, up from 47.2% in September 2008), there has been a concurrent weakening in employment outcomes for higher education graduates in recent years.

The share of NEET (not in employment, education, or training) among Australian youth has been consistently below the OECD average. In Australia about 600 000 of 16-29 year olds are NEET in 2015 and females are more likely to be NEET than young males (OECD, 2017[2]). And yet, the average share of NEET for 20-to 24-year olds in Australia has been considerably lower than the average of other OECD countries since 2000 and has been declining until 2008. The average share of NEET among 15- to 19-year-olds followed a similar pattern up to 2008, when there was a 2 percentage point increase in the share of NEET, and since then the average share of NEET in Australia in this age range is very close to or higher than the OECD average. In 2017, about 12% of 20- to 24-year-olds and about 5.4% of 15- to 19-year-olds were NEET in Australia. Apprenticeship or traineeship opportunities can be particularly important for NEET and disengaged youth to re-connect to the labour market (OECD, 2017[2]).

Figure 1.5. Australian youth not in employment, education, or training (NEET): 2000-17

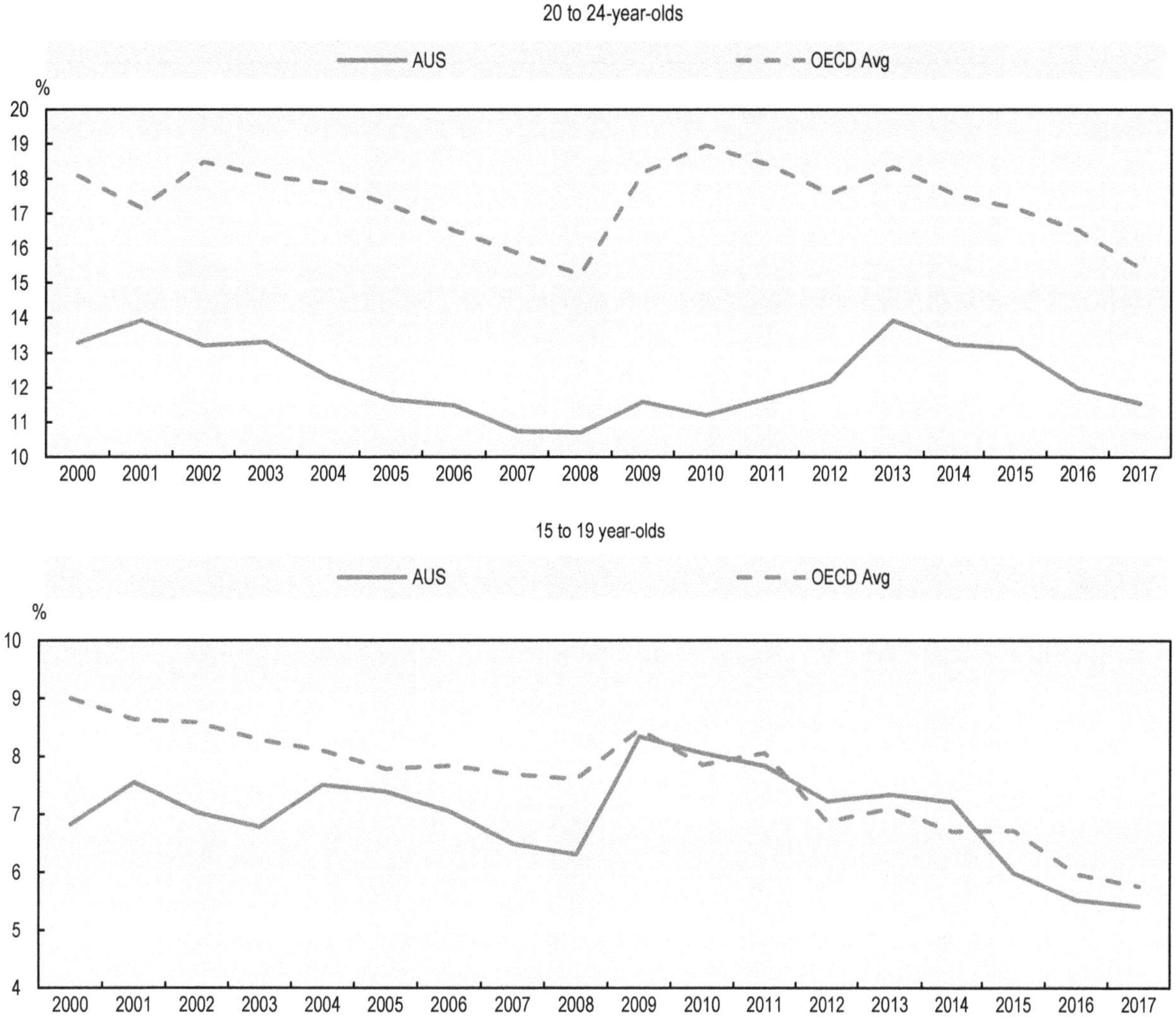

Source: OECD (2018), Youth not in employment, education or training (NEET) (indicator). doi: 10.1787/72d1033a-en (accessed on 1 October 2018).

StatLink https://doi.org/10.1787/888933931732

Regional differences

Over the last few decades, some states were consistently strong performers while others continued to face challenges in terms of high unemployment rates. The average unemployment rate varies across states with a few of them consistently having relatively higher or lower unemployment rates than others (Figure 1.6).

Figure 1.6. Unemployment rate (%, 15 and older) by state and territory, 2000-17

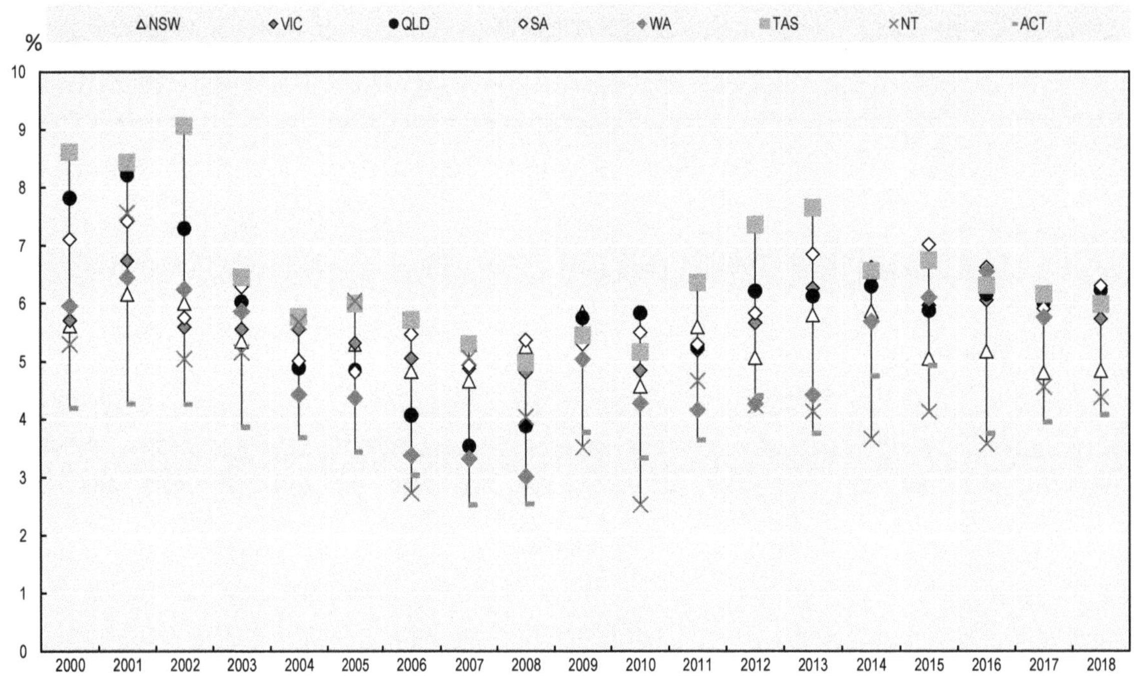

Note: 2018 includes data from January to February only
Source: ABS Labour Force Survey.

StatLink https://doi.org/10.1787/888933931751

As shown in Figure 1.6, Tasmania has been most frequently ranked as the state with the highest unemployment rate since 2000 followed by South Australia in the recent years after the mining boom has waned. In contrast, the Australian Capital Territory (ACT) consistently had the lowest unemployment rate in the early 2000s and after the crisis, the Northern Territory began to perform strongly. Given this consistent trend of certain states performing strongly or weakly due to either macro-level changes or local labour market conditions, it would be important to better understand the sources of regional variation.

Tasmania (6.2%) had the highest unemployment rate among Australian states and territories in 2017, followed by Victoria (6.1%), and Queensland (6%) (Figure 1.7). Given that Victoria and Queensland are one of the top ranked states with respect to projected employment growth in the next five years, policy makers should pay close attention to skill shortages and skill mismatches among these states that have projected growth but also high unemployment rates.

Figure 1.7. Unemployment rate (%, 15 and older) by state and territory, 2017

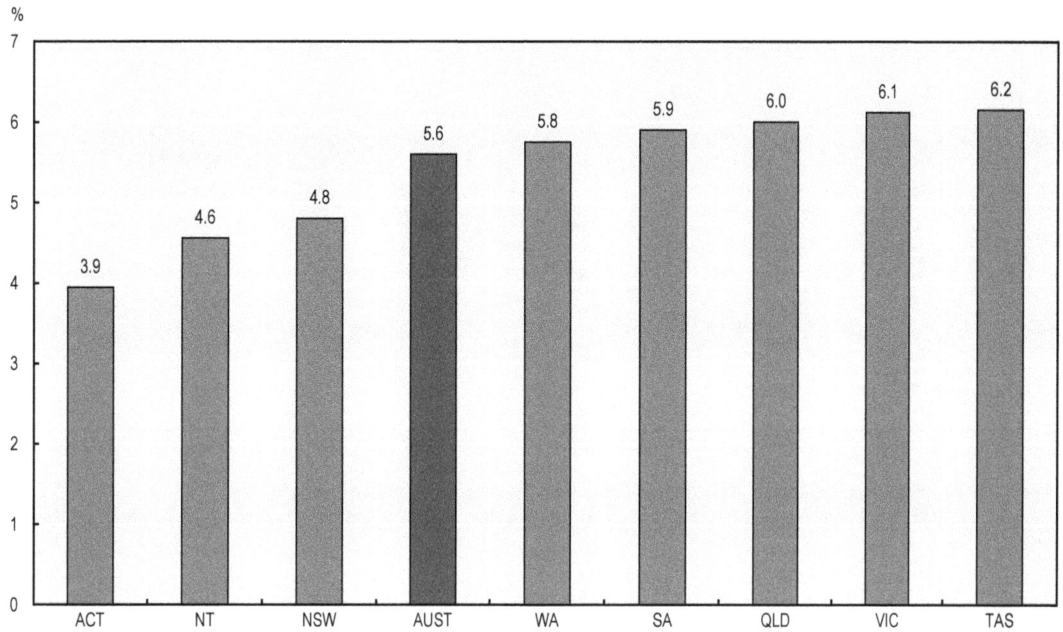

Source: ABS Labour Force Survey.

StatLink https://doi.org/10.1787/888933931770

While the variation of state and territory level unemployment rates or the gaps between states and territories have not changed significantly over the course of the last two decades, significant changes have shaped labour market conditions across states and territories over the same period. For instance, states such as Western Australia and Queensland, and the Northern Territory, which previously performed well, have been significantly affected by the end of the mining boom. Western Australia's unemployment rate reached a pre-GFC low of 2.7% in August 2008 but has been on a broad upward trend since mid-2012, due to the end of the mining boom, reaching a post-GFC peak of 6.8% in March 2018. While there has been an improvement in Western Australia's labour market more recently, the unemployment rate remains elevated, at 6.4% in May 2018.

South Australia and parts of Victoria have been affected by the closure of the car manufacturing industry in Australia in recent years. South Australia's unemployment rate reached a pre-GFC trough of 4.4% in August 2008 but rose to a post-GFC high of 8.2% in June 2015. There has been some improvement in labour market conditions over the last year, with the state's unemployment rate declining to 5.6% in May 2018.

The New South Wales and Victoria labour markets have strengthened over the last year due to construction and strong population growth.

Employment trends and projections by industry

Over the last two decades, employment in service industries in Australia has shown considerable growth (Figure 1.8) compared to employment trends in other industries.

Figure 1.8. Employment in services sector, Australia 1998-2017

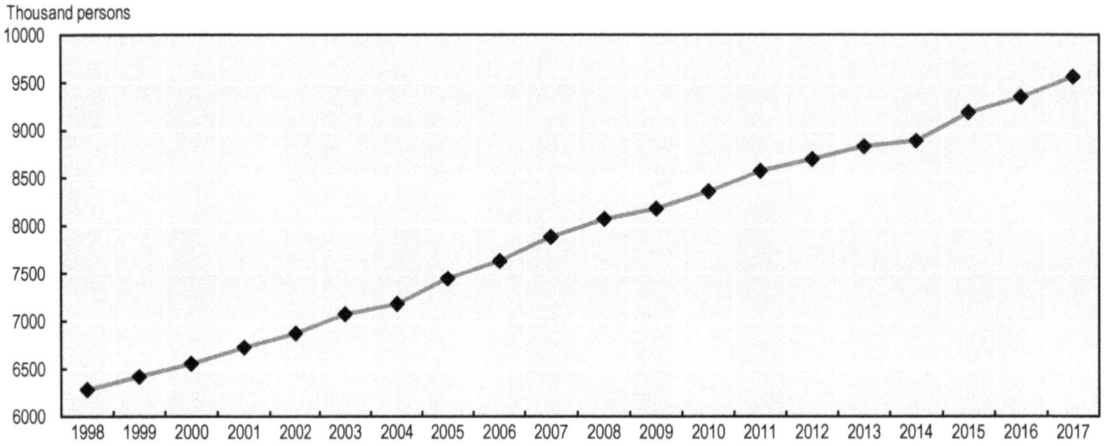

Note: This indicator is seasonally adjusted and it is measured in thousands of people.
Source: OECD (2018), Employment by activity (indicator). doi: 10.1787/a258bb52-en (Accessed on 1 October 2018).

StatLink https://doi.org/10.1787/888933931789

The recent report Australian Jobs 2018, published by the Australian Government Department of Jobs and Small Business, highlights various employment characteristics in Australia by industry and region. Five industries in Australia offer over 1 million jobs each and together comprise almost half of Australian employees. According to the most recent Australian Jobs publication, the top five largest industries (in terms of number of employed persons) are Health Care and Social Assistance (1 663 900), Retail Trade (1 286 900), Construction (1 167 200), Professional, Scientific and Technical Services (1 033 000), and Education and Training (1 024 300) (Australian Government Department of Jobs and Small Business, 2018[3]).

Over the five years to May 2018, 17 of the 19 broad industries recorded growth in employment, with employment growth in these industries far offsetting declines in employment in the remaining two industries (Figure 1.9). Employment grew in a range of service industries over the period, with the largest recorded in Health Care and Social Assistance (up by 309 500), Construction (178 800), Professional, Scientific and Technical Services (139 500), Education and Training (113 200) and Accommodation and Food Services (105 400). By contrast, a decrease in employment was recorded in Wholesale Trade (down by 63 900) and Mining (30 000). The lower level of employment in the Mining industry reflects the passing of the Mining investment boom, with the transition eased by a favourable dollar and commodity prices.

Figure 1.9. Changes in employment by industry, Australia, five years to May 2018 ('000)

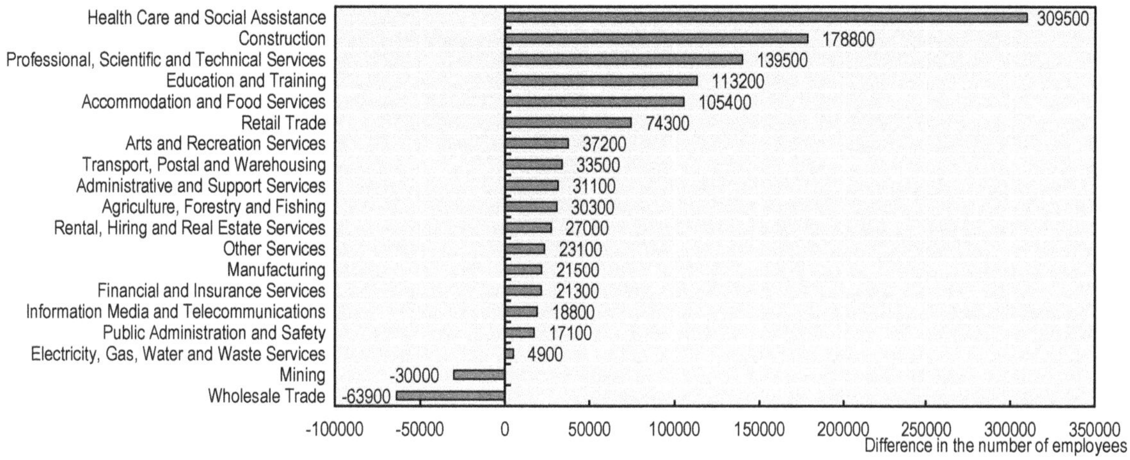

Source: ABS Labour Force Survey, trend.

StatLink https://doi.org/10.1787/888933931808

Looking forward, the shift in the Australian labour market towards service industries is projected by the Australian Government Department of Jobs and Small Business to continue over the five years to May 2022 (Figure 1.10). Health Care and Social Assistance is projected to make the largest contribution to employment growth (increasing by 250 500 or 16.1%), followed by Professional, Scientific and Technical Services (126 400 or 12.5%), Construction (120 700 or 10.9%) and Education and Training (116 200 or 12.0%). Together, these four industries are projected to provide 61.5 per cent of total employment growth over the five years to May 2022. By contrast, declines in employment are projected for Manufacturing, Electricity, Gas, Water and Waste Services and Agriculture, Forestry and Fishing. For all states and the Northern Territory, the largest growth in employment is projected in the Health Care and Social Assistance industry. In the Australian Capital Territory, the Health Care and Social Assistance industry is projected to record the second largest increase in employment. As such, many skills associated with the industry are likely to face substantial increases in demand.

In line with current employment levels in the Health Care and Social Assistance industry, the largest increases in employment in the industry are projected in the more populous states of News South Wales, Victoria and Queensland (Table 1.1). By contrast, a decline in employment in Manufacturing is projected across most states and territories, with the largest falls expected in Victoria and New South Wales.

Figure 1.10. Projected employment growth by industry, Australia, five years to May 2022 ('000)

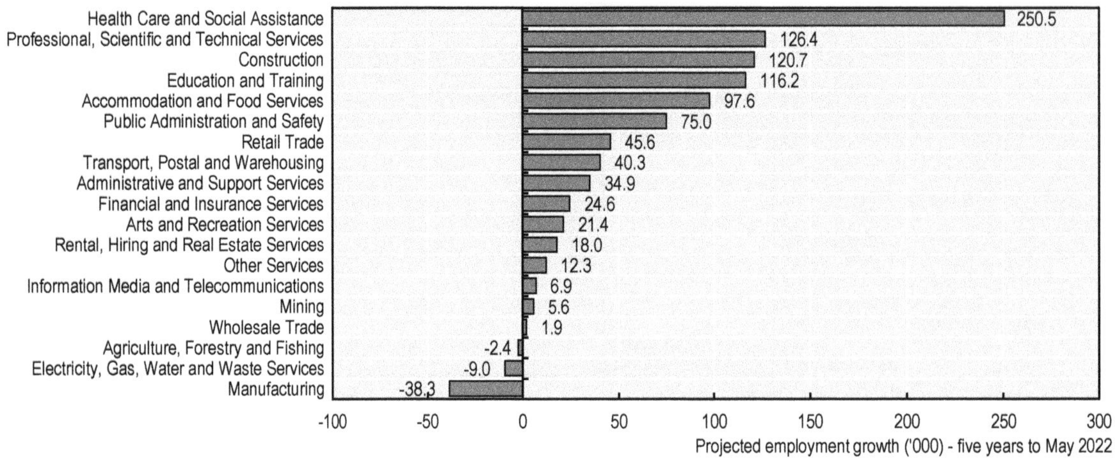

Source: Australian Government Department of Jobs and Small Business, employment projections, five years to May 2022.

StatLink https://doi.org/10.1787/888933931827

Table 1.1. Projected employment growth by industry and by state and territory, five years to May 2022 ('000)

Industry	NSW	VIC	QLD	SA	WA	TAS	NT	ACT	AUSTRALIA
Agriculture, Forestry and Fishing	-3.4	1.4	-1.4	0.4	0.7	0.0	0.0	0.0	-2.4
Mining	0.0	0.2	0.1	0.1	4.9	0.0	0.3	0.0	5.6
Manufacturing	-12.6	-15.6	-3.3	-3.9	-2.8	-0.2	0.0	0.0	-38.3
Electricity, Gas, Water and Waste Services	-2.8	-2.4	-2.3	0.2	-1.6	-0.2	0.2	-0.1	-9.0
Construction	45.9	33.4	20.2	5.6	12.8	1.4	0.5	1.0	120.7
Wholesale Trade	2.5	-0.2	0.8	-1.0	0.0	-0.2	0.1	0.0	1.9
Retail Trade	15.9	22.0	2.6	0.7	2.4	1.6	0.3	0.1	45.6
Accommodation and Food Services	21.4	29.4	25.6	1.4	15.6	1.5	1.4	1.4	97.6
Transport, Postal and Warehousing	8.9	12.7	12.0	1.4	4.4	0.5	0.2	0.2	40.3
Information Media and Telecommunications	5.4	-1.5	1.9	0.0	1.1	0.0	0.0	0.0	6.9
Financial and Insurance Services	11.7	6.7	3.5	0.5	1.9	0.2	0.0	0.0	24.6
Rental, Hiring and Real Estate Services	8.7	5.2	1.9	0.7	0.8	0.1	0.2	0.3	18.0
Professional, Scientific and Technical Services	55.6	37.8	18.3	2.8	7.1	0.9	0.4	3.4	126.4
Administrative and Support Services	11.0	12.8	2.9	3.0	4.1	0.6	0.3	0.2	34.9
Public Administration and Safety	22.3	18.4	18.3	4.6	8.1	0.4	0.1	2.8	75.0
Education and Training	39.8	34.9	21.8	5.8	9.3	1.4	1.2	2.0	116.2
Health Care and Social Assistance	82.8	71.9	48.7	14.9	21.8	5.3	2.0	3.2	250.5
Arts and Recreation Services	7.8	3.8	3.7	1.6	3.6	0.1	0.3	0.4	21.4
Other Services	-1.2	3.6	6.1	0.3	3.1	0.2	0.0	0.1	12.3

Note: The employment projections are derived from best practice time series models that summarise the information that is in a time series and convert it into a forecast. The projections are made by combining forecasts from autoregressive integrated moving average (ARIMA) and exponential smoothing with damped trend (ESWDT) models, with some adjustments made to take account of research undertaken by the Department of Jobs and Small Business and likely future regional developments. The projections are also made to be broadly consistent with the national ANZSIC Industry projections published in September 2017.
New national level industry projections have been released for the five years to May 2023, but not used here to retain comparability with state/territory projections.
Source: Australian Government Department of Jobs and Small Business, 2018 Employment Projections

Different factors contribute towards these employment trends and projections. A steady rise of the elderly population in Australia is linked to the rise of employment growth in the health care service sector. The share of people over the age of 65 has nearly doubled in Australia in the last four decades. The percentage of elderly population (relative to total working age population 15-64) in Australia increased from 8% in 1970 to 15% in 2014 and the growth is expected to continue. Such demographic changes in Australia in conjunction with increases in migrant flow will influence what kinds of skills are needed or in shortage as well as other labour market trends.

Brief overview of state labour market conditions

New South Wales (NSW)

According to the most recent available data, NSW is the largest employing state in Australia where nearly one in three Australian employees reside (Australian Government Department of Jobs and Small Business, 2018[5]). Most of the workforce is concentrated around Sydney. In line with employment at the national level, the largest employing industries in NSW in May 2018 were Health Care and Social Assistance, Retail Trade, Professional Scientific and Technical Services and Construction. It is projected that the largest growing states in terms of employment over the five years to May 2022 will be NSW, followed by Victoria and Queensland (see Figure 1.11).

Figure 1.11. Projected employment growth by state and territory ('000)

Total (industry), by state/territory

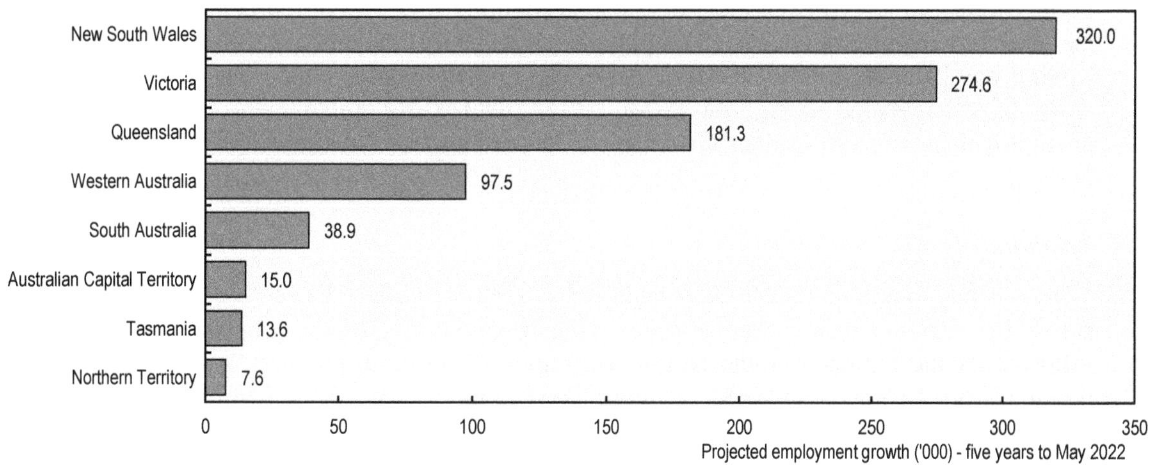

Source: Australian Government Department of Jobs and Small Business, employment projections, five years to May 2022.

StatLink https://doi.org/10.1787/888933931846

Victoria (VIC)

Victoria, the second largest employing state in Australia, added the most new jobs over the past five years, and this employment growth is likely to continue in the next few years (see Figure 1.11 above). As in NSW, Health Care and Social Assistance was the largest employing industry in Victoria, followed by Retail Trade, Professional, Scientific and Technical Services and Construction. Most of the workforce is concentrated in the greater

Melbourne area, which has the most educated workforce within the state (Australian Government Department of Jobs and Small Business, 2018[5]).

Queensland (QLD)

Queensland had about 2.5 million employees in November 2017 and it is the third largest employing state in Australia. Unlike New South Wales and Victoria, employment is more spread out across the region in Queensland. About one in two jobs are in Brisbane and 13% are located in the Gold Coast area. Health Care and Social Assistance is the largest employing industry in the state, followed by Retail Trade and Construction. Compared to the other states and the national average, workers in Queensland are less likely to have a bachelors' degree but more likely to have a Certificate III or higher VET qualification (Australian Government Department of Jobs and Small Business, 2018[5]).

South Australia (SA)

South Australia has a relatively small workforce compared to other Australian states. Nearly 80% of the jobs in South Australia are concentrated in the Greater Adelaide area. Workers in South Australia are slightly more likely to be working part-time than the national average, and less likely to have post-school qualifications (Australian Government Department of Jobs and Small Business, 2018[5]).

Western Australia (WA)

About 1.3 million employees work in Western Australia and about 80% of jobs are concentrated in the state capital, Perth. In May 2018, there were 100 000 people employed in the Mining industry in Western Australia, accounting for 7.4% of total employment in the state (compared with 1.9% of employment nationally). Notably, 43.4% of national Mining employment was in Western Australia. Labour market conditions in Western Australia strengthened in the year to May 2018, with rising employment and a falling unemployment rate (Australian Government Department of Jobs and Small Business, 2018[5]).

Tasmania (TAS)

Tasmania has about 245 000 workers and is more regionally diverse (jobs are most spread across the regions) than the other states. Hobart holds 45% of the jobs in Tasmania, followed by the Launceston and North East region (27%) and the West and Northwest region (21%). Tasmanian workers are more likely to have a Certificate III or higher VET qualification than a bachelor's degree (or higher). The share of older workers (55 or older) in Tasmania is 23%, which is higher than the national average of 19%. Over the year to January 2018, employment rose in Tasmania, although this was mostly due to a rise in part-time employment. Tasmanian youth workforce had a higher unemployment rate of 14% in January 2018 compared to the national average of 12% (Australian Government Department of Jobs and Small Business, 2018[5]).

Northern Territory (NT)

The Northern Territory has about 135 000 workers but recently employment growth has been subdued and employment fell over the year to May 2018. The largest employing industry in the Northern Territory in May 2018 was Health Care and Social Assistance, followed by Public Administration and Safety (Australian Government Department of Jobs and Small Business, 2018[5]).

Australian Capital Territory (ACT)

In May 2018, the largest employing industry in the Australian Capital Territory was Public Administration and Safety, accounting for 28.5% of total employment in the territory (compared with 6% of employment nationally). In addition, the Australian Capital Territory has the most educated workforce in Australia with nearly three quarters of employees holding a post-school qualification (Australian Government Department of Jobs and Small Business, 2018[5]).

Skill shortages and recruitment difficulties

International evidence

According to the 2018 Talent Shortage Survey conducted by ManpowerGroup across 43 countries and territories, surveying around 40 000 hiring managers, almost half the employers surveyed across the globe report talent shortages (ManpowerGroup, 2018[6]). As shown in Figure 1.12, there was a sharp rise before the Global Financial Crisis in the share of managers reporting talent shortages. This has been steadily decreasing for Australia since 2008, while the global average has gradually increased.

For the first time since 2006, compared to the average in this survey Australia today faces a lower share of managers reporting such difficulties as compared to the global average. About 34% of Australian employers reported that they have difficulties filling positions. One in four employers says filling skilled trade roles is harder this year than last. Among the reasons for talent shortages, Australian employers cite the lack of applicants (25%), the lack of required hard skills (21%) and the lack of experience (19%) as the main reasons for difficulty in filling vacancies in 2018. In order to tackle this challenge, over three quarters of employers are offering training and development to existing staff and about 60% of managers try to recruit from outside of the traditional talent pool (older/younger employees). Another 51% of managers in Australia reported exploring alternative sourcing strategies such as hiring temporary workers.

Similarly, ManpowerGroup surveyed a representative sample of 1 503 Australian employers for the ManpowerGroup Employment Outlook Survey (the first quarter of 2018). Looking at regional differences, employers in New South Wales reported the highest hiring intentions with a 21% increase in staffing levels in the first quarter of 2018 followed by Tasmania and Queensland. Except for Victoria, the overall employment outlook of employers strengthened compared to 2015 across all regions in Australia (ManpowerGroup, 2018[7]).

Figure 1.12. Percentage of employers facing difficulty filling jobs, Manpower Talent Survey 2018

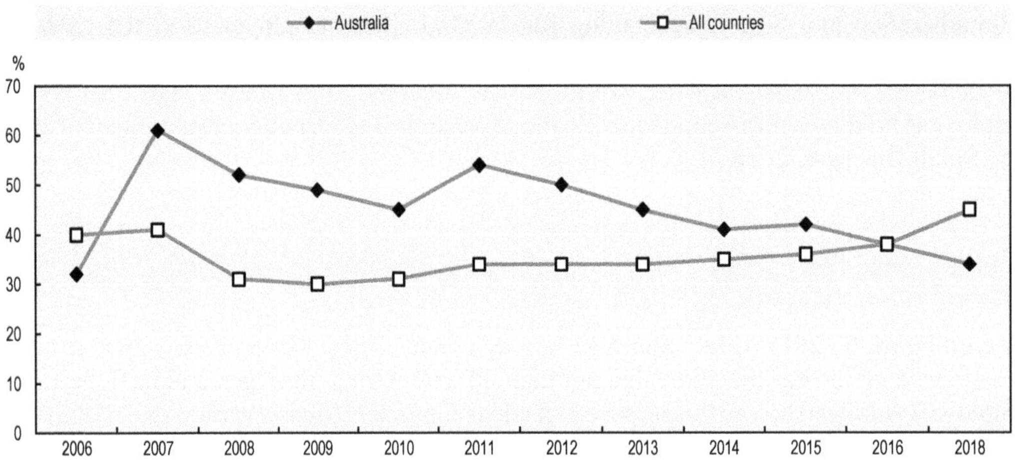

Source: ManpowerGroup Talent Shortage Survey 2018.

StatLink https://doi.org/10.1787/888933931865

As shown in Figure 1.13, in 2018, Japan has the highest percentage of managers reporting skills shortages across 43 countries, followed by Romania (81%), Taiwan (78%), Hong Kong (76%) and Bulgaria (68%). Australia has 34% of hiring managers reporting skills shortages, which is slightly below the average across countries. Across all participating countries, skilled trades, including electricians, welders, mechanics and more, as well as sales representatives, engineers, drivers and technicians, have ranked among the top five hardest roles to fill for the past ten years. A similar pattern holds true for Australia. For the past ten consecutive years, hiring managers in Australia report skilled trade positions (electricians, carpenters, welders, bricklayers, plasters, plumbers and more) as the most difficult jobs to fill.

Figure 1.13. Cross-country comparison: Percentage of employers having difficulty filling jobs

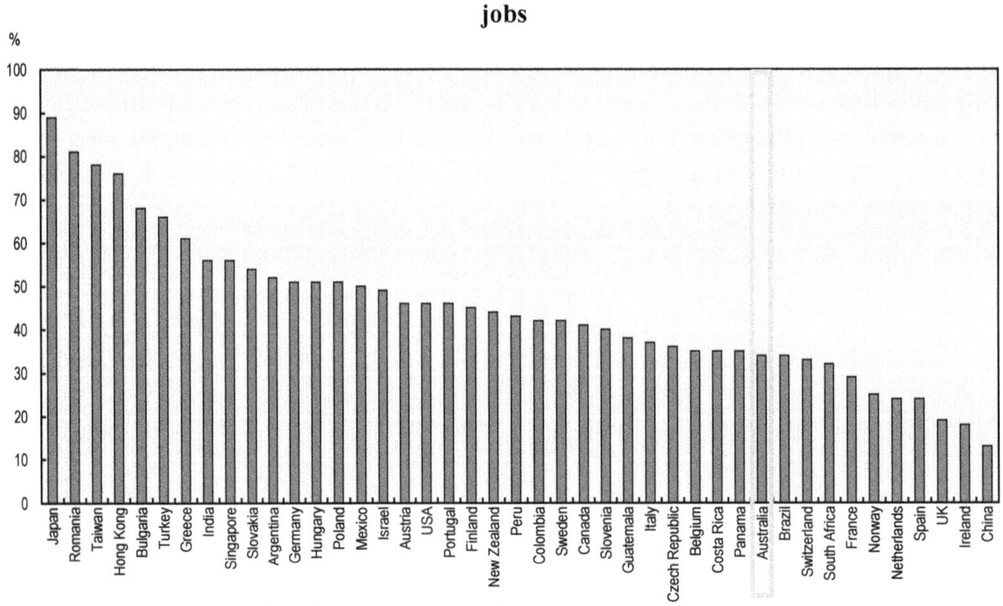

Source: ManpowerGroup Talent Shortage Survey 2018.

StatLink https://doi.org/10.1787/888933931884

Evidence from OECD Skills for Jobs database

Looking at other sources, the OECD Skills for Jobs Database provides useful information about skill shortages and skill surpluses as well as information regarding the qualification and field-of-study mismatch. As shown in Figure 1.14, many of the skills, knowledge areas and abilities are in shortage. In Australia, knowledge in Education and Training has the highest need followed by Health services and Mathematics and Sciences. Some of the skills that tend to have shortages include verbal and reasoning abilities, basic process skills, systems skills and complex problem solving skills. However, despite the fact that so many skills, knowledge areas and abilities are in shortage, in reality the intensity of the shortages in Australia is low relative to other countries in the OECD Skills for Jobs Database.

Figure 1.14. Skills shortages and surpluses, Australia, 2016

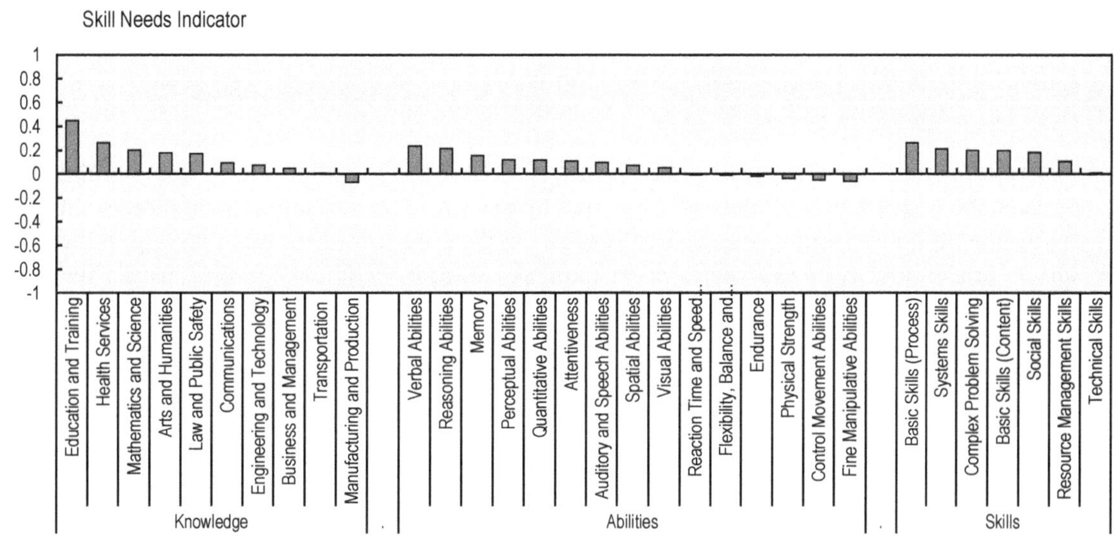

Note: Positive values indicate shortages while negative values indicate surpluses. Basic Skills (Process) refer to those skills that contribute to the more rapid acquisition of knowledge and skill across a variety of domains (e.g. critical thinking, active learning, etc.). Basic Skills (Content) refer to foundational structures needed to work with and acquire more specific skills in a variety of domains (e.g. reading comprehension, listening, writing, speaking, basic math and science).
Source: OECD Skills for Jobs database 2017; OECD, Getting Skills Right: Australia, 2018

StatLink https://doi.org/10.1787/888933931903

In addition to skill shortages and surpluses, it is important to consider skills mismatch and its trends to gauge and respond to the needs of employers. Skills mismatch can indicate different types of mismatch in the labour market. Mismatch of qualifications can occur when a worker has a higher or lower than necessary qualification (education attainment) for the job. Field-of-study mismatch occurs when a worker works in a different field than the one specialised in education. Skills mismatch can occur when a worker's skills are greater or less than the level required to perform the job (OECD, 2018[8]).

The most recent Skills for Jobs database suggests that on average about 35% of workers across OECD countries were mismatched by qualification in 2017 (OECD, 2018[8]). According to OECD PIAAC data, about 40% of workers experience field-of-study mismatch and about 11% are overqualified within their field and 13% are overqualified outside of their field (Montt, 2017[9]). About 39% of Australian workers experience qualification mismatch, which is just above the OECD average (OECD, 2018[8])

Such mismatches can incur costs to individuals, firms, and the economy as a whole (OECD, 2018[8]). Field-of-study mismatch may lead to a lower wage (or wage penalty) if the workers are overqualified (Montt, 2017[9]). Workers with over-qualifications may suffer from lower job satisfaction and the extent is greater for those who are both over-skilled and overeducated (Sloane, 2014[10]).

Recent evidence indicates that variations of skills mismatch across countries are related to differences in public policies. While it is difficult to draw a causal conclusion, after controlling for individual's socio-demographic and job characteristics, having well-designed product and labour markets are correlated with lower skills mismatch (Mcgowan and Andrews, 2015[11]). Some of the factors that contribute to improving skills matching of individuals include greater participation in lifelong learning, better management quality and flexible wage negotiations (Mcgowan and Andrews, 2015[11]).

Evidence from the Programme for the International Assessment of Adult Competencies (PIAAC) data

The results from the Survey of Adult Skills (PIAAC) suggest that adults in Australia possess above-average proficiency in the literacy and problem solving in technology-rich environments components compared with adults in the other countries participating in the survey, and around average proficiency in numeracy skills (OECD, 2012[12]). However, the average performance masks the variation and distribution of skills among Australian adults. According to the most recent PIAAC data from Australia (2011-12), one in five Australian adults has low literacy and/or numeracy skills (low skills defined by not reaching the Level 2 proficiency out of a scale of 1 to 5). Furthermore, there is a considerably large gap between those who are most and least proficient in numeracy and literacy (OECD, 2017[2]).

There is also a gender gap in terms of field of study and performance in numeracy skills. Females are less likely to go in to fields of study that need mathematical and numeracy skills such as science, technology, engineering and mathematics (STEM) and perform poorly in numeracy compared to males (OECD, 2017[2]). Nonetheless, Australian adults perform strongly in problem solving skills in technology-driven environments as well as strong computer and ICT skills across all age groups (OECD, 2017[2]). This can be particularly important in the coming years as new technology and developments will continue to evolve and alter the nature of work and work environment.

Regional differences

Skills demand and labour market characteristics vary across different states and territories. The Department of Jobs and Small Business (DJSB) assesses and publishes skill shortages by state and occupation groups. Based on the definition from the DJSB, skill shortages occur when "employers are unable to or have considerable difficulty filling vacancies, or significant specialised skill needs within that occupation, at current levels of remuneration and conditions of employment and in reasonably accessible locations" (Australian Government Department of Jobs and Small Business, 2018[13]).

Several occupation groups commonly face skill shortages across Australian states and territories, including occupations in the field of automotive and engineering trade workers, design, engineering, science and transport professionals, and health professionals. Occupation group that face skill shortages the most (in terms of the absolute number of occupation listed) are technicians and trade workers (Table 1.2), particularly in New South Wales, Victoria, and South Australia. This is in line with the ManpowerGroup Talent Shortage Survey, where managers in Australia ranked skilled trade positions as the most difficult positions to fill in vacancies for the past ten years.

Table 1.2. Occupation groups with skill shortages, 2017

	Professionals	Technicians and trade workers	Community and personal service workers
New South Wales	Civil Engineering Professionals, Mechanical Engineer, Medical Diagnostic Radiographer, Sonographer, Physiotherapist	Motor mechanics, Structural steel and welding trades workers, fitter, metal machinist, panelbeater, vehicle painter, carpenters and joiners, painting trades worker, fibrous plasterer, plumbers, cabinetmaker, Electrician (general), Air conditioning and refrigeration mechanic, baker, chef	n/a
Victoria	Civil Engineering Professionals, Mechanical Engineer, Medical Diagnostic Radiographer, Sonographer, Physiotherapist	Motor mechanics, sheetmetal trades worker, structural steel and welding trades workers, metal mechanist, panelbeater, vehicle painter, bricklayer, carpenters and joiners, fibrous plasterer, plumbers, cabinetmaker, air conditioning and refrigeration mechanic, baker	n/a
Queensland	Civil Engineering Professionals, Sonographer, Physiotherapist	Motor mechanics, Sheetmetal trades worker, fitter, panelbeater, painting trades worker, cabinetmaker, air conditioning and refrigeration mechanic, baker	n/a
South Australia	Surveyor, Civil Engineering Professionals, Occupational Therapist, Physiotherapist	Architectural draftsperson, motor mechanics, diesel mechanic, metal fabricator, metal machinist, panelbeater, vehicle painter, bricklayer, painting trades worker, fibrous plasterer, cabinetmaker, air conditioning and refrigeration mechanics, baker	n/a
Western Australia	Medical Diagnostic Radiographer, Sonographer, Physiotherapist	Panelbeater, Vehicle Painter	n/a
Tasmania	n/a	Diesel mechanic, metal machinist, panelbeater, vehicle painter, bricklayer, plumbers	n/a
Northern Territory	Accountants, Medical Diagnostic Radiographer, Hospital/Retail Pharmacsit, Occupational Therapist, Physiotherapist, Midwife	Sheetmetal trades worker, structural steel and welding trades workers, vehicle painter, bricklayer, carpenters and joiners, electrician, baker	Enrolled nurse
Australian Capital Territory	Civil Engineering Professionals, Sonographer, Hospital/Retail Pharmacist	Motor mechanics, structural steel and welding trades workers, panelbeater, painting trades worker, fibrous plasterer, plumbers, cabinetmaker, air conditioning and refrigeration mechanic	Childcare worker (diploma)

Source: Australian Government Department of Jobs and Small Business, National, state and territory skill shortage information

However, the absence of skill shortages of particular occupation groups is not equivalent to a perfect skills match. Another interesting indicator on skills demand and supply is recruitment difficulty by different occupation groups. Recruitment difficulties occur when some employers have difficulty filling vacancies for an occupation. Unlike skill shortages, there may be an adequate supply of skilled workers but some employers are unable to attract and recruit sufficient suitable workers for reasons which include: the specific experience or specialist skill requirements of the vacancy; differences in hours of work required by the employer and those sought by applicants; or particular locational or transport issues (Australian Government Department of Jobs and Small Business, 2018[13]).

Table 1.3. Occupation groups facing recruitment difficulty, 2017

	Professionals	Technicians and trade workers	Community and personal service workers
New South Wales	n/a	n/a	n/a
Victoria	Civil engineering professionals (for experienced professionals in specialised projects or specific industry settings), architect, mechanical engineer (extensive experience and a high degree of specialisation in a specific sector), registered nurses	Metal fitters and machinists	n/a
Queensland	n/a	Carpenters and joiners, plumbers, electrician (general)	n/a
South Australia	Accountants	Carpenters and joiners	n/a
Western Australia	Civil engineering professionals	Structural steel and welding trades workers	n/a
Tasmania	Architect, Medical Diagnostic Radiographer, Registered Nurses	Motor Mechanics, metal fitters and machinists, carpenters and joiners	n/a
Northern Territory	n/a	Plumbers (experienced maintenance plumbers), chef	Enrolled nurse
Australian Capital Territory	Early childhood (pre-primary school) teacher	n/a	n/a

Note: "Recruitment difficulty" occurs when there may be an adequate supply of skilled workers, but some employers have difficulty filling vacancies for an occupation for reasons including the specific experience or specialist skill requirements of the vacancy; differences in hours of work required by the employer and those sought by applicants; or particular locational or transport issues.
Source: Australian Government Department of Jobs and Small Business, National, state and territory skill shortage information.

The Internet Vacancy Index (produced by the Australian Government Department of Jobs and Small Business) provides another useful indicator of changes in demand for occupations. Over the year to August 2018, job advertisements rose in six of the eight occupational groups, with the strongest gains recorded for Professionals (up by 8.5%), Technician and Trade Workers (7.7%), and Clerical and Administrative Workers (6.2%) (Australian Government Department of Jobs and Small Business, 2018[14]).

Job advertisements rose in four states and the Australian Capital Territory. Tasmania recorded the strongest annual rise (up by 17.7%, albeit from a low base), followed by Western Australia (13.4%), and Victoria (8.2%).

Following a low point in October 2013, the Internet Vacancy Index in August 2018 was 43 300 job advertisements (or 31.0%) higher than October 2013.

Figure 1.15. Number of job advertisements by state and territory

August 2006 – August 2018

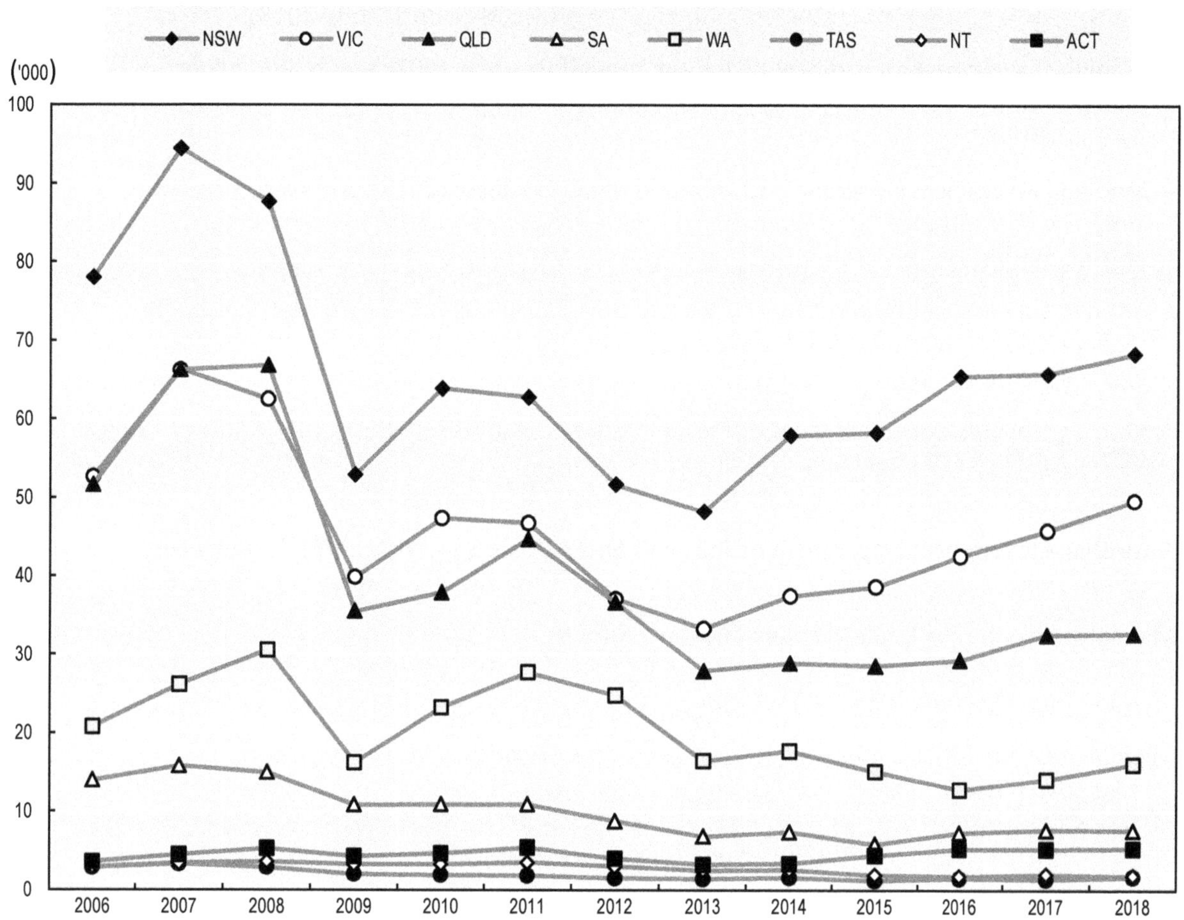

Note: In thousands. Data is from August each year.
Source: Australian Government Department of Jobs and Small Business.

StatLink https://doi.org/10.1787/888933931922

References

Australian Government Department of Jobs and Small Business (2018), *Australian Jobs 2018*, https://www.jobs.gov.au/australian-job-publication (accessed on 15 July 2018). [5]

Australian Government Department of Jobs and Small Business (2018), *Australian Jobs Infographics*, https://www.jobs.gov.au/news/australian-jobs-2018-now-available (accessed on 15 July 2018). [3]

Australian Government Department of Jobs and Small Business (2018), *National, state and territory skill shortage information*, https://www.jobs.gov.au/national-state-and-territory-skill-shortage-information. [13]

Australian Government Department of Jobs and Small Business (2018), *Ratings Summary - Labour Market Analysis of Skilled Occupations*, https://www.jobs.gov.au/national-state-and-territory-skill-shortage-information. [15]

Australian Government Department of Jobs and Small Business (2018), *Vacancy Report: August 2018*, Australian Government, http://lmip.gov.au/default.aspx?LMIP/GainInsights/VacancyReport. [14]

Australian Government Department of Jobs and Small Business (2018), *2018 Employment Projections*, http://lmip.gov.au/default.aspx?LMIP/GainInsights/EmploymentProjections. [4]

ManpowerGroup (2018), *2018 Talent Shortage Survey*, https://go.manpowergroup.com/hubfs/TalentShortage%202018%20(Global)%20Assets/PDFs/MG_TalentShortage2018_lo%206_25_18_FINAL.pdf?t=1539038418916. [6]

ManpowerGroup (2018), *ManpowerGroup Employment Outlook Survey Australia*, ManpowerGroup, https://www.manpowergroup.com/wps/wcm/connect/0606dc20-a968-4c72-8fb8-0877ee528c3f/AU_MEOS_1Q18.pdf?MOD=AJPERES&CACHEID=0606dc20-a968-4c72-8fb8-0877ee528c3f (accessed on 26 February 2018). [7]

Mcgowan, M. and D. Andrews (2015), *The Future of Productivity: Main Background Papers Skill Mismatch and Public Policy in OECD Countries*, OECD, https://www.oecd.org/eco/growth/Skill-mismatch-and-public-policy-in-OECD-countries.pdf (accessed on 17 April 2018). [11]

Montt, G. (2017), "Field-of-study mismatch and overqualification: labour market correlates and their wage penalty", *IZA Journal of Labor Economics*, Vol. 6/1, p. 2, http://dx.doi.org/10.1186/s40172-016-0052-x. [9]

OECD (2018), *Getting Skills Right: Australia*, OECD. [8]

OECD (2017), *Building Skills for All in Australia: Policy Insights from the Survey of Adult Skills*, OECD Publishing, Paris, http://dx.doi.org/10.1787/9789264281110-en. [2]

OECD (2017), *OECD Economic Surveys: Australia*, http://www.oecd.org/eco/surveys/economic-survey-australia.htm (accessed on 12 February 2018). [1]

OECD (2012), *Survey of Adult Skills First Results: Australia.* [12]

Sloane, P. (2014), "Overeducation, skill mismatches, and labor market outcomes for college graduates", IZA, http://dx.doi.org/10.15185/izawol.88. [10]

Chapter 2. The evolving role of vocational education and training at the national and local level

This chapter describes the recent trends in VET and apprenticeship training in Australia at the local level. Over the last decade, the share of young Australians earning a tertiary degree, including Short-cycle, Bachelor, Master's, Doctoral or equivalent degrees, has been increasing and consistently higher than the OECD average. This chapter also summarises recent reforms related to VET and apprenticeship programmes. Different trends related to apprenticeship training are highlighted. The share of Australians in-training and completion of apprenticeship training has declined in the recent years. Some of the states that experienced the most decline in absolute numbers are New South Wales, Victoria and Queensland.

Education attainment in Australia

Over the last two decades, the share of 25 to 34 year olds with tertiary education (defined as ISCED Level 5 qualifications and above[1]), has been increasing in Australia. In 2017, one in two 25-to 34-year-old Australians had tertiary education, which is higher than the average across OECD countries (Figure 2.1).

Figure 2.1. Share of 25 to 34 year olds with tertiary education, including Short-cycle, Bachelor, Master's and Doctoral or equivalent degrees, in Australia

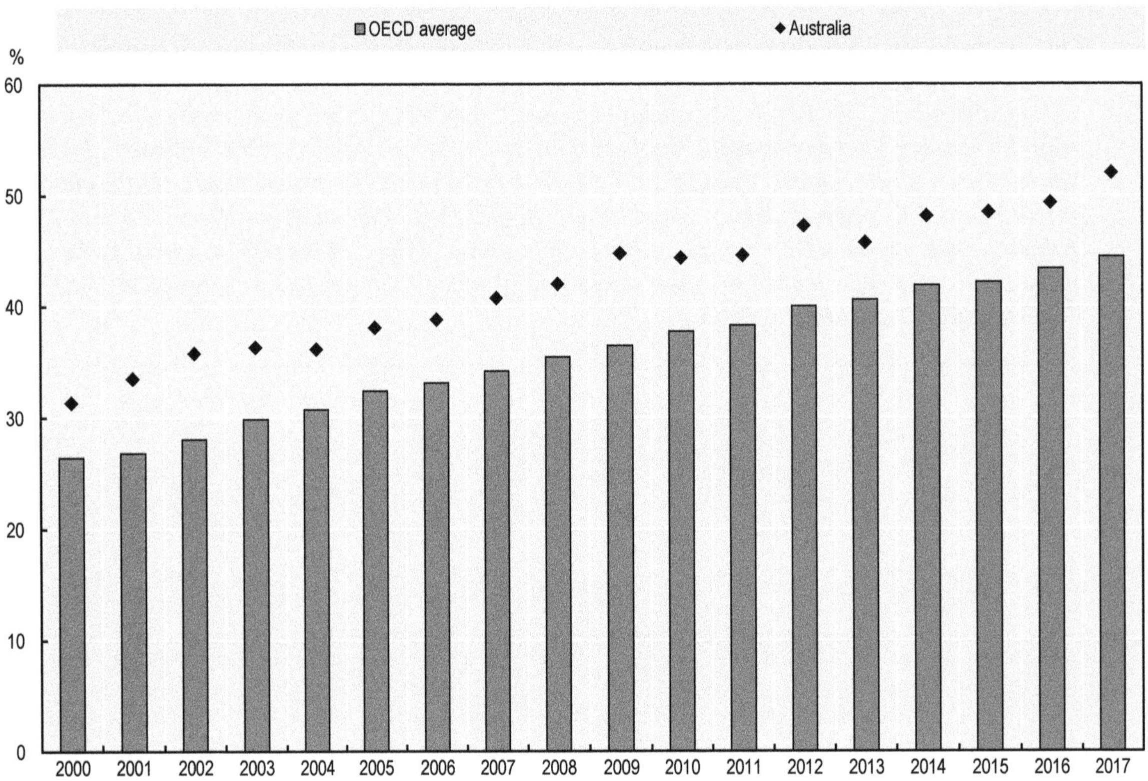

Note: Population with tertiary education is defined as those having completed the highest level of education, by age group. This includes both theoretical programmes leading to advanced research or high skill professions such as medicine and more vocational programmes leading to the labour market. The measure is percentage of same age population. As globalisation and technology continue to re-shape the needs of labour markets worldwide, the demand for individuals with a broader knowledge base and more specialised skills continues to rise.
Source: OECD (2018), Population with tertiary education (indicator). doi: 10.1787/0b8f90e9-en (Accessed on 09 October 2018).

StatLink https://doi.org/10.1787/888933931941

Within secondary and post-secondary level, many students in most OECD countries tend to pursue general programmes as opposed to vocational programmes.

On average, a lower percentage of students enrol in upper secondary vocational programmes than in general programmes in conjunction with lower completion rates for vocational education. About 54% of people from OECD countries will graduate from an upper secondary general programme during their lifetime. Comparatively, the share of people earning a vocational degree during their lifetime is about 44% on average across OECD countries (OECD, 2017[15]).

Figure 2.2 illustrates the cross-country variations in programme orientation among 25-34 year olds whose highest level of education is upper secondary or post-secondary non-tertiary. This category includes general programmes designed to prepare students for further education, as well as VET designed to lead directly to the labour market. Many European countries such as Austria, Denmark, Finland, France, Germany, Italy, the Netherlands, Poland, Slovakia, Slovenia, and Switzerland have a substantial share of students whose highest level of education is in vocational education programme relative to general programme (Figure 2.2). This can reflect the tradition and development of VET systems and network in different countries. Australia and New Zealand have a similar share of students seeking a vocational education and general education programme at this level of education. In Australia, VET is one of the largest education sectors with an estimate of 4.2 million working age people (15 to 64 years) taking some form of VET in 2015 (Atkinson and Stanwick, 2016[16]).

Within vocational education programmes, certain fields of specialisation have attracted more students in recent years. In 2015, 34% of graduates in vocational programmes on average across OECD countries had a specialisation in engineering, manufacturing and construction compared to 27% of Australian graduates specialising in these fields. This OECD average goes down to 12% for business, administration and law (26% for Australia), 17% for services (11% for Australia), and 12% for health and welfare (26% for Australia) (OECD, 2017[15]).

Figure 2.2. Percentage of 25-34 year-olds whose highest level of education is upper secondary or post-secondary non-tertiary, including general programmes and VET, by programme orientation (2016)

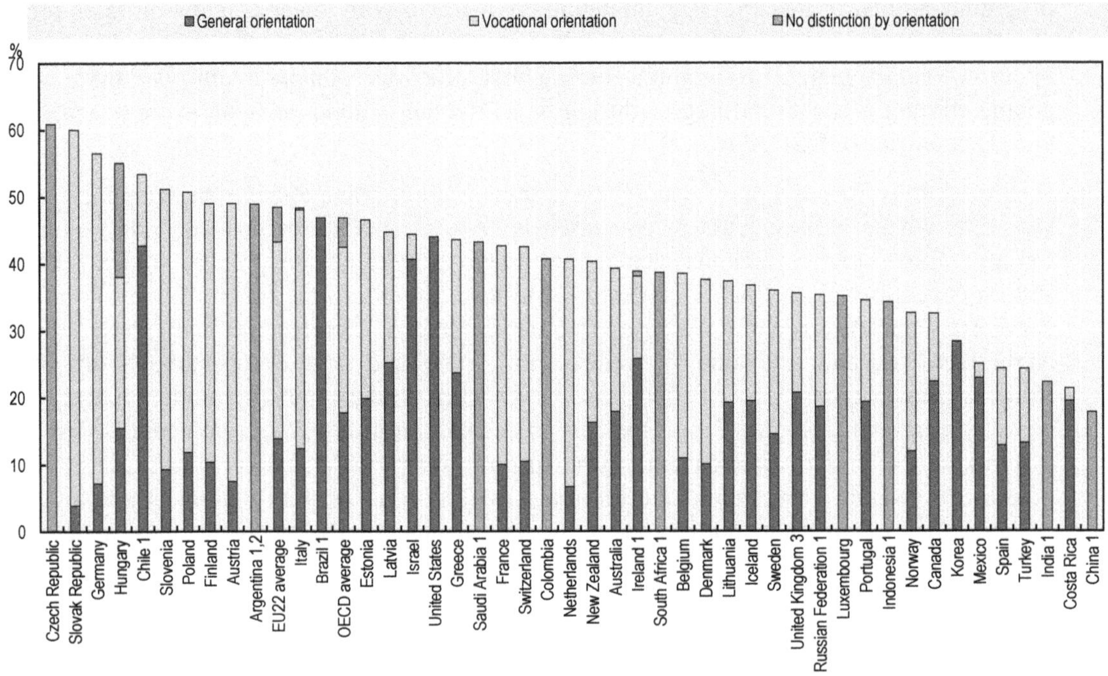

Note: 1. Year of reference differs from 2016. Refer to the Table A1.1 for more details. 2. Data should be used with caution. See Methodology section for more information. 3. Data for upper secondary attainment include completion of a sufficient volume and standard of programmes that would be classified individually as completion of intermediate upper secondary programmes (16% of adults aged 25-64 are in this group).
Source: OECD / ILO / UIS (2017), Education at a Glance Database, http://stats.oecd.org/. See Source section for more information and Annex 3 for notes (www.oecd.org/education/education-at-a-glance-19991487.htm).

StatLink https://doi.org/10.1787/888933931960

Impact of quality vocational education and training (VET) system

VET is an important part of the education system in most OECD countries and can play a crucial role in preparing youth for a smooth transition to work and develop relevant skills for the labour market needs (OECD, 2017[15]). Having a well-developed and high quality VET system and apprenticeship programmes can foster skills development and enhance opportunities to find jobs for youths, particularly disengaged youths (OECD, 2014[17]).

This correlation between VET and employability is strong at the upper secondary level, especially when the skills developed are in line with what the industry and labour market demands. Evidence shows that among young adults with upper secondary programmes as their highest level of education, those who graduated from vocational training tend to have higher employment rates and lower inactivity rates (OECD, 2017[15]). Figure 2.3 demonstrates this relationship to some extent among 25 to 34 year olds. For most of the countries, those with a tertiary qualification, including Short-cycle, Bachelor, Master's, Doctoral or equivalent degrees, tend to have the highest rate of employment but those with vocational training tend to have a higher employment rate than those with general education. Australian young adults with vocational training tend to have a similar employment rates as those with a tertiary qualification.

Figure 2.3. Employment rates of 25 to 34 year olds, 2016

By educational attainment and programme orientation

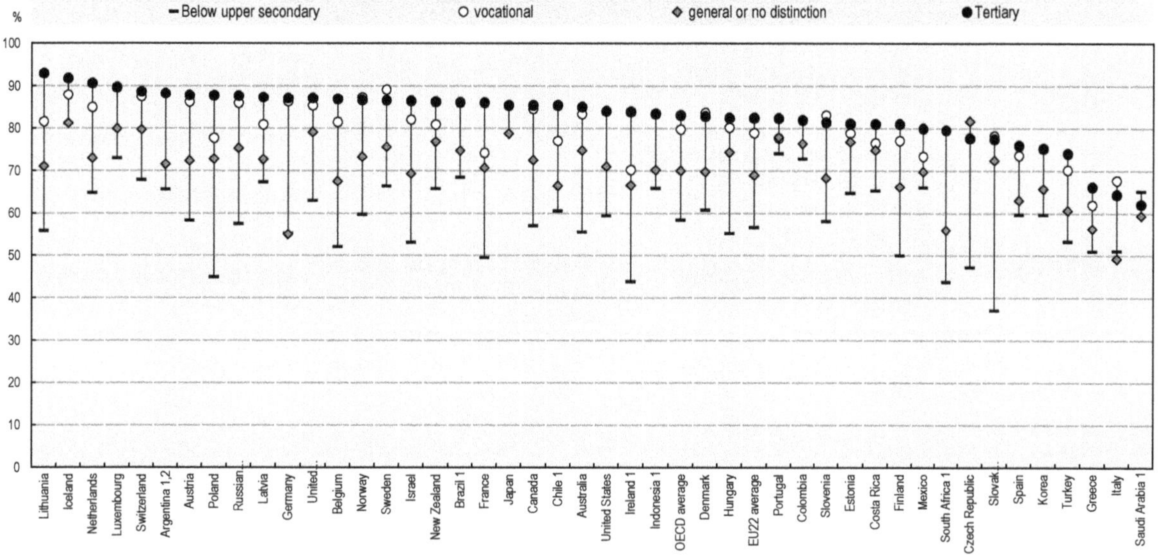

Note: Countries are ranked in descending order of the employment rate of 25-34 year-olds with tertiary education, including Short-cycle, Bachelor, Master's, Doctoral or equivalent degrees. The label upper secondary or post-secondary non-tertiary (general or no distinction) refers to "general" for countries with a value for "vocational" and to "no distinction" for the others.

Source: OECD / ILO (2017), Education at a Glance Database, http://stats.oecd.org/. See Source section for more information and Annex 3 for notes (www.oecd.org/education/education-at-a-glance-19991487.htm).

StatLink https://doi.org/10.1787/888933931979

Overview of the Australian VET system

Australia's vocational education and training (VET) system involves different layers of government where the national common framework is developed together with the state/territory and federal governments. Each state and territory government adopts the common framework into their own VET system. The Australian VET system has a nationally agreed system in place for qualifications recognition and quality assurance of training providers. It is also industry-centered because various industry stakeholders identify the required training outcomes (OECD, 2014[18]).

Table 2.1 illustrates the different levels of government and stakeholders involved in the vocational education system as well as other regional economic and employment policy.

Table 2.1. Institutional mapping at the national and state/territory level

	Overall decision-making	Regulation of VET	Industry liaison
National	Australian Government agency responsible for VET, currently the Department of Education and Training COAG Industry and Skills Council (collaboration between the Australian Government and state and territory governments)	Australian Skills Quality Authority	Australian Industry and Skills Committee Industry Reference Committees Skills Service Organisations
State/territory	State and territory government departments responsible for VET	State/territory training authority. Two state VET regulators with limited powers.	Skills board or industry training advisory bodies

Source: Productivity Commission of the Australian Government, 2018, Report on Government Services 2018; and author's elaborations.

National level

At the national level, the Australian Government Department of Education and Training is responsible for national policies and programmes that help Australians access quality and affordable early child care and childhood education, school education, higher education, vocational education and training, international education and research. This department is responsible for post-school education and training through three distinct, but closely interrelated, areas: 1) provide policy advice and support to the Minister, underpinned by research, analysis and evaluation; 2) national programme management; 3) working relationships with state and territory governments, industry, education and training providers, and other stakeholders.

Australia's VET system is led by a council made up of Australian, state and territory government ministers responsible for industry and skills. The Council of Australian Governments (COAG) Industry and Skills Council (CISC) provides leadership and direction for the sector. In May 2015, CISC established the Australian Industry and Skills Committee (AISC) to provide industry advice to CISC and to approve nationally recognised training packages for implementation.

Both the federal and state/territory-level governments have roles in the governance, regulation and funding of Australia's national VET system.

About 4 400 registered training organisations (RTOs) deliver VET in Australia through public Technical and Further Education (TAFE) institutes, universities, secondary schools, private training providers, enterprises, industry organisations, community-based providers and other government organisations.

As the national VET regulator, the Australian Skills Quality Authority (ASQA) is responsible for regulating RTOs against the VET Quality Framework. The framework includes standards for RTOs, the Australian Qualifications Framework, and requirements for fit and proper persons, financial viability and risk. ASQA is also responsible for registering all RTOs that offer courses to overseas students (Australian Skills Quality Authority, 2018[20]). Victoria and Western Australia have not referred their VET sector regulatory powers to ASQA, the national regulator, and maintain their own regulatory bodies. These two state VET regulators have limited powers to regulate RTOs that operate solely in those jurisdictions offering training and assessment services only to domestic students. The three VET regulators are responsible for accrediting courses that sit outside the training package development and endorsement process.

Training packages are a key feature of Australia's national VET system. A training package is a set of nationally endorsed standards and qualifications for recognising and assessing peoples' skills in a specific industry, industry sector or enterprise (Australian Industry and Skills Committee, 2016[21]).

The development of training packages follows a consultative approach, where industry is consulted on an ongoing basis to identify skills and training needs. Industry Reference Committees (IRCs) are the formal channel for considering industry skills requirements in the development and review of training packages and providing advice to the AISC (Australian Industry and Skills Committee, 2017[22]). IRC members are industry leaders who understand the skills needs of their sector, industry or occupation, and are supported by Skills Services Organisations (SSOs). SSOs are independent, professional service organisations that support IRCs to gather industry intelligence for the sectors they represent to inform training product development and review, ensuring training meets the needs of employers across Australia. IRCs are responsible for producing Industry Skills Forecasts, proposed Schedules of Work, Cases for Endorsement of training packages, and other submissions for consideration by the AISC. They also promote the use of VET in the sectors they represent. There are currently over sixty IRCs supported by six SSOs.

The AISC has also established a number of specific-purpose IRCs to provide an explicit focus on understanding the skilling requirements in sectors expecting to experience significant growth and significant workforce skilling requirements as a result of key industry or government priorities. These IRCs focus on identifying gaps in training products across tertiary education sectors to strengthen workforce development and support pathways for workers within and across industry sectors.

The AISC approves training packages for implementation, which are then formally endorsed by all skills ministers through CISC. According to its Terms of Reference, the AISC may also provide industry advice on the implementation of national training policies; providing direction to research priorities within the VET sector; provide industry advice to COAG on training provider and regulator standards and co-ordinate industry engagement in relevant COAG meetings.

Council of Australian Governments (COAG)

This is the peak intergovernmental forum in Australia, comprising the Prime Minister, State Premiers, Territory Chief Ministers and the President of the Australian Local Government Association (ALGA). Its role is to initiate, develop and monitor the implementation of policy reforms (including in VET) that are of national significance and which require co-operative action by Australian governments.

Australian Skills Quality Authority (ASQA)

ASQA is the national regulator for Australia's VET sector, responsible for: registering training providers; ensuring that organisations comply with the conditions and standards for registration, including by carrying out compliance audits; accrediting VET courses.

State/territory and local levels

Each Australian state and territory government has a training authority with the main responsibilities of providing strategic direction to VET, through the development and implementation of policies; planning and reporting on VET strategies; purchasing training on behalf of their government, and administering funding and financial incentives for VET within the state/territory; regulating the VET sector locally, through quality assurance and performance monitoring; and supporting and advising training organisations, employers and the community on VET issues.

The state/territory training authorities are directly responsible for delivering policy, strategy and funding for skills development and training at the local level. One example of a common VET policy at the state level is the definition of priority skills lists, specific to each state, which are periodically revised through industry and community consultation and labour market research, and determine VET qualifications that are eligible for Government subsidies.

State training authorities consult and gather intelligence from industry and peak bodies to inform policy and strategy directions, and sometimes work in partnership with local community organisations to co-develop and fund skills development programmes. The case studies in the following chapters will show an example of a workforce development strategy that entails partnerships between state government departments and local industry (See Chapter 5), and another of a pre-employment programme which is an initiative of a local community organisation, co-developed and funded by a state training authority (See Chapter 6).

New South Wales (NSW)

The NSW Department of Industry, through Training Services NSW, is the State Training Authority, leading strategic policy, planning, funding, and regulating the VET sector in the state. It is also responsible for contract management of training providers and for implementing quality assurance and performance monitoring.

The NSW Skills Board is responsible for providing independent, high-level, strategic advice on the NSW VET system and for overseeing major reforms of the system. It receives administrative support from Training Services NSW. The Board has established two reference groups, which will provide input on specific matters relevant to VET and skills reform: an Industry Reference Group and a Provider Reference Group. For example, the Industry Reference Group will be consulted on matters such as the implementation of reforms to the VET system in NSW; labour market trends, skills shortages and current and future skills and workforce development needs; quality assurance and regulatory issues in VET, including industry engagement in independent validations of assessment; the performance of the VET system in delivering on industry skills priorities in NSW; areas for possible research and innovation, and emerging issues for the VET sector.

Industry Training Advisory Bodies (ITABs) are autonomous, industry-based bodies, contracted by the NSW Department of Industry, to represent their specific industries in:

- identifying industry skill needs, priorities and skills development issues for funded training in NSW;
- promoting training to industry and assisting in the take up of funded training;
- advising the Department about apprenticeship and traineeship arrangements;
- advising on the development, review and implementation of training packages;
- supporting the delivery of VET to school students.

They may also advise RTOs on registration processes and accreditation and review of courses, on a fee for service basis. There are currently 11 ITABs in NSW, covering major industry areas, and their board members represent significant enterprises, employers and unions of their respective industry sectors[2].

Table 2.2. Recent VET initiatives and reforms in NSW

	Year	
Smart and Skilled	2014 - continuing	This VET reform has been structured to allow people to learn the skills they need to find a job and make progress in their careers. This reform includes: • Entitlement for entry level training including (and up to) certificate III targeted support for higher level qualifications (NSW Skills Lists defines subsidised courses) • Better information, informed choice along with quality improvement • Recognition of the role and function of TAFE NSW as the public provider • Increased support for regions and equity groups
Access to Smart and Skilled expanded (2016 onwards)	2016 - continuing	The main goal of this initiative is to enhance the access to training for youth via: • fee-free scholarships for socially disadvantaged • scholarships to students in STEM related training and vocational qualifications • Places for job training that will help the delivery of the National Disability Insurance Scheme and free VET for people with a disability
$14.7 million to Boost Agri Skills	2017 - continuing	Partner with peak grain and cotton industry bodies, the NSW government's goal is to provide $14.7 million over the next three years for subsidised training to help the NSW agricultural sector recruit new talents and upskill existing workers. Will help industry with skills development in farm machinery, business management, emerging technologies (drones and satellite data) in agriculture.
Regional VET Pathways Programme	2015 - continuing	This initiative helps about 1000 15-to 19-year-olds who are NEET to find opportunities in education, employment, and training. The programme focuses on five regions: Richmond-Tweed region; Mid-North Coast region; Capital region; Central West region; New England North West region

Source: NCVER, 2018, VET Knowledge Bank Timeline of Australian VET policy initiatives 1998-2017 | VOCEDplus, the international tertiary education and research database, http://www.voced.edu.au/vet-knowledge-bank-timeline-australian-vet-policy-initiatives-1998-2017 (accessed on 03 May 2018).

Tasmania

Skills Tasmania is Tasmania's State Training Authority (part of the Department of State Growth), responsible for developing strategies and providing support, advice, and funding for the VET system within the state. Skills Tasmania developed an Industry Advice Framework in late 2013 following the dissolution of the industry-led Skills Tasmania Board on 30 June 2013. The Framework established the Endorsed Strategic Partners, which are industry associations with the role of providing high-level strategic advice on training and workforce development on behalf of their constituencies. At the end of May 2016, there were 13 Endorsed Strategic Partners representing specific industry groups.

Skills Tasmania has also hosts consultation sessions to gather advice on training and workforce development priorities and needs from a range of actors: 'Regional Industry Leaders' Forums', through which business leaders in regional areas are consulted; 'Community Conversations', for individuals, small businesses and community groups; and 'RTO Conversations' sessions. Skills Tasmania also employs Workforce Development Consultants, who consult with industry representatives to gather intelligence for informing skills development strategies and planning.

Table 2.3. Recent VET policy reforms in Tasmania

Name	Year	Description
Training Entitlement Policy	2014 - continuing	For all Tasmanians who did not already have a certificate III or higher qualifications were given entitlement to a government subsidised training place in a certificate III qualification. This is in line with the requirements of the National Training Entitlement as agreed between governments in the National Partnership Agreement for Skills Reform.
Training and Workforce Development Act	2013 – continuing	The main objective of this legislation is to establish workforce development and training system to foster skilled workforce that can contribute to social and economic progress in Tasmania. The proposed system consists of: • VET including Tasmania's traineeship and apprenticeship system • Other training or skills and workforce development • Foundation skills The legislation also established 1) Tasmanian Traineeships and Apprenticeships Committee (TTAC) to have accessible systems and procedures for training contracts and vocational placements; 2) TasTAFE, a new entity public VET provider in Tasmania that merges Tasmanian Polytechnic and the Tasmanian Skills Institute.
Training and Work Pathways Programme launched	2016 – continuing	The aim is to provide support towards employment and access to training for Tasmanians facing disadvantage. The programme brings a series of grant for targeted projects that address specific themes and barriers and support people facing disadvantage and barriers towards VET participation and finding employment.

Source: NCVER, 2018, VET Knowledge Bank Timeline of Australian VET policy initiatives 1998-2017 | VOCEDplus, the international tertiary education and research database, http://www.voced.edu.au/vet-knowledge-bank-timeline-australian-vet-policy-initiatives-1998-2017 (accessed on 03 May 2018).

Queensland

The Department of Education and Training (DET) is Queensland's State Training Authority, leading strategic policy, planning, funding, and regulating the VET sector in the state. Jobs Queensland is an independent statutory entity established by the Queensland Government with the aim of giving a strong voice for industry and regions on skills priorities and long-term workforce planning. To achieve that, Jobs Queensland engages with industry, industry associations and peak bodies, regions, communities, employers and unions to:

- provide strategic advice on future skills needs, helping government to prioritise its investment in VET;
- provide strategic advice on apprenticeships and traineeships in order to enable them to be a key pathway to employment and a skilled workforce;
- undertake workforce planning and development initiatives;
- commission research into future industry needs.

Table 2.4. Recent VET reforms and initiatives in Queensland

Name	Year	Description
Great skills. Real Opportunities	2013-2018	Five-year action plan to improve access and completion of skills training necessary to find a job. Training would focus on closely aligning skills need and training, targeted investment based on industry guidance, and widening access and choice for students.
Rescuing TAFE	2015 - continuing	The goal of this initiative is to support the TAFE sector and provide high-quality training in Queensland by restoring TAFE Queensland as the public provider of VET through $34 million government investment during the three consecutive years.
What's Next (Out-of-home care) OOHC Fund	2017 - continuing	This initiative is for young people in Queensland who have been in out-of-home care (OOHC) to have access to VET to raise job prospects and opportunities. Youth will be able to receive assistance from: • What's Next pathways officer to navigate the VET system and to make informed choices • Assessing options and skills to find a suitable job and career path • Financial support to meet the cost of training • Payment for other training-related expenses
Back to Work Regional Employment Package	2016 – continuing	This package aims to increase employment opportunities in regional Queensland. • $80 million support for employers to regional workers, particularly among the disadvantaged (long-term unemployment, youth, mature-age job seekers), and indigenous population. • $10 million for the Certificate III Guarantee Boost programme to increase access to subsidised courses • $10 million for Back to Work officers who are knowledgeable about the local economic condition and employers who can connect local employers and job seekers through Regional Employment Networks.

Source: NCVER, 2018, VET Knowledge Bank Timeline of Australian VET policy initiatives 1998-2017 | VOCEDplus, the international tertiary education and research database, http://www.voced.edu.au/vet-knowledge-bank-timeline-australian-vet-policy-initiatives-1998-2017 (accessed on 03 May 2018).

Table 2.5. VET reforms with a targeted local focus in NT, ACT, VIC, SA, and WA.

Name	Region	Date	Description
Job Plan 3 (Skilling Territorians)	Northern Territory	2016 - continuing	Building upon the two previous job plans to foster job growth and skills development in the territory, Job Plan 3 consists of workforce employment and training strategy and key priority areas for the territory.
Skilled Capital Initiative	Australian Capital Territory	2015 - continuing	This entitlement programme has been developed as part of the National Partnership Agreement on Skills Reform (NPASR). This involved comprehensive support system to help students access the training and complete the programme as well as consultations to identify the needs of diverse group of students. Given the concerns of high dropout rates among RTOs and the need for more support for those going through certificate II level qualifications, subsidy amount has been subsequently changed.
Regional and Specialist Training Fund	Victoria	2017 - continuing	This is a targeted for funding stream under Skills First to meet local industry and community training needs in Victoria. The funding will help training providers to deliver training for selected courses in specific regions via higher subsidies and grant payments. In addition, this will help students to access training and develop skills that are relevant to the local industry.
SA's Industry Priority Qualifications Survey	South Australia	2016 - continuing	SA is conducting this survey and to identify and meet the future skills priorities and accordingly align the system. Findings from this survey and industry consultations help align the public investment to identify and train youth with relevant skills for the local industry and economy.
Future Skills WA	Western Australia	2014 - continuing	Future Skills WA (Now Jobs and Skills WA) is the way WA government prioritises its investments on courses that help prepare people with the skills that are in high demand. This initiative offers a guaranteed spot for eligible students with subsidies to enrol in courses with state priority qualifications.

Source: NCVER, 2018, VET Knowledge Bank Timeline of Australian VET policy initiatives 1998-2017 | VOCEDplus, the international tertiary education and research database, http://www.voced.edu.au/vet-knowledge-bank-timeline-australian-vet-policy-initiatives-1998-2017 (accessed on 03 May 2018).

The evolving role of Apprenticeships

The number of apprentices and trainees in Australia has seen an increase in the early 2000s, particularly in metal and vehicle and building sectors. These two sectors still has the largest number of apprentices and trainees. However, since around 2012 several trade occupations, which include Technicians and Trades Workers as classified by the Australian Bureau of Statistics (2013[24]) saw a decline in the number of apprentices and trainees, especially in the metal and vehicle industry (Figure 2.4). This is in line with the skills shortage in occupations relevant to these industry sectors in Australia.

Figure 2.4. Number of Australians in apprenticeship or traineeship by trade occupation

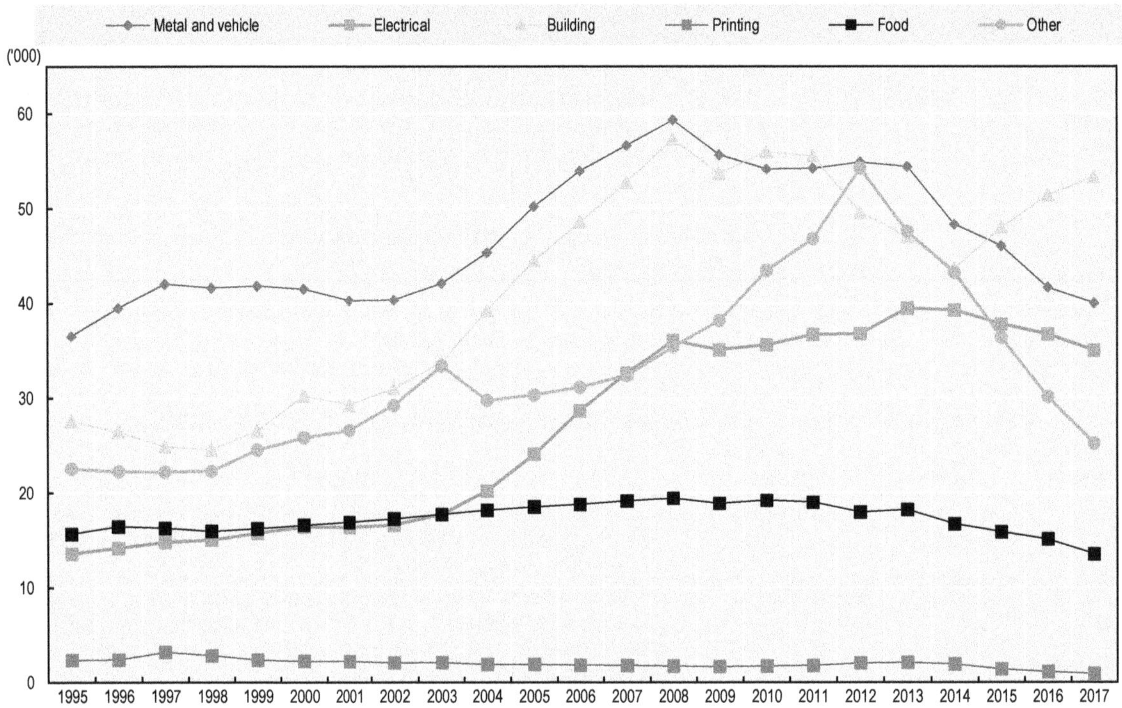

Source: NCVER, 2017, Historical time series of apprenticeships and traineeships in Australia, from 1963, NCVER, Adelaide.

StatLink https://doi.org/10.1787/888933931998

Across different states and territories, New South Wales has had the highest number of apprentices and trainees followed by Victoria and Queensland. However, in the last five years, the number of apprentices and trainees has sharply dropped among these three states as well as South Australia. This could reflect an increase in the drop-out or cancellation rate and/or low commencement rates of apprenticeships among these states and territories. Given the projected increase in employment in many of these states with declining apprentices, boosting apprenticeship opportunities at the local level can help reduce the skill shortages in the states and territories.

Figure 2.5. Number of Australians in apprenticeship or traineeship by state and territory

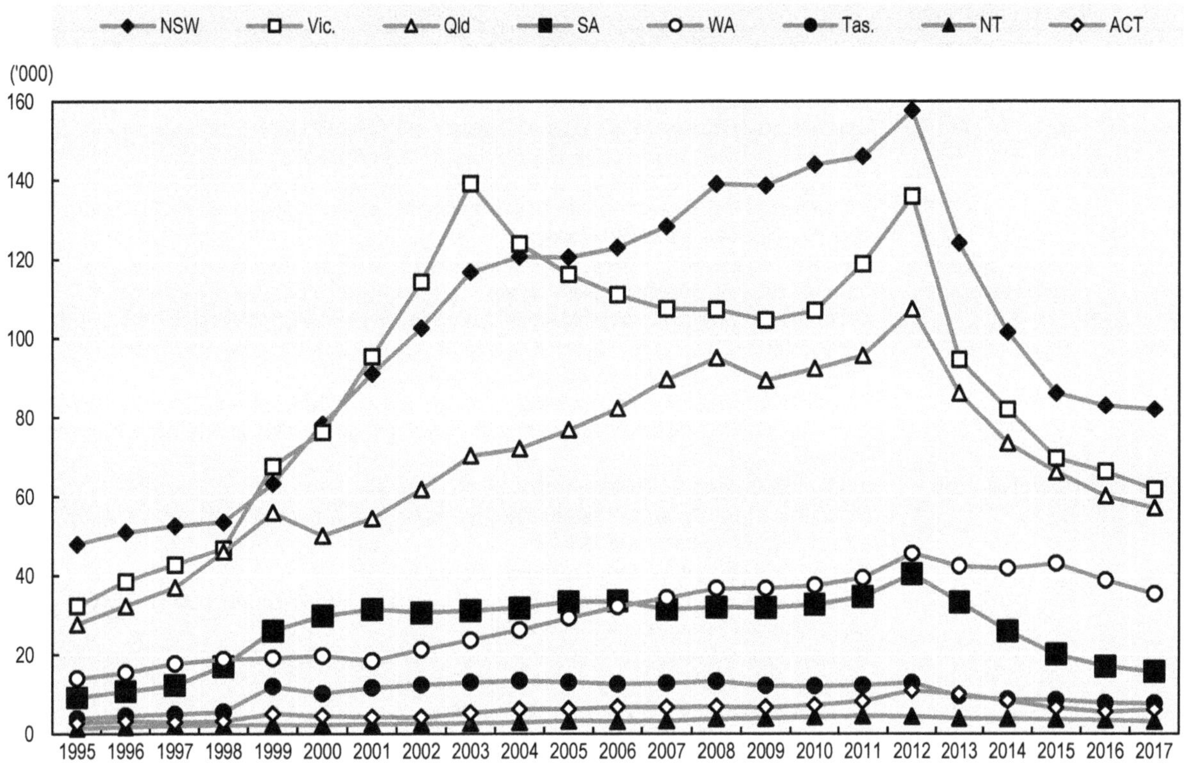

Source: NCVER, 2017, Historical time series of apprenticeships and traineeships in Australia, from 1963, NCVER, Adelaide.

StatLink https://doi.org/10.1787/888933932017

Table 2.6. Relevant reforms and initiatives in Australia regarding apprenticeships

Year	Name or State/Territory	Description
2012	Commencement initiatives	Commencement incentives for existing worker apprenticeships and traineeships not on the National Skills Needs List (NSNL) removed from 1 July 2012 Commencement and completion incentives for diploma and advanced diploma qualifications not leading to aged care, child care or enrolled nursing removed from 23 October 2012. Commencement incentives for part-time apprenticeships and traineeships removed from 23 October 2012. The following cohorts unaffected: part-time, certificate III/IV qualifications on NSNL, school-based apprenticeships and traineeships, and part-time diploma and advanced diploma qualifications leading to aged care, child care or enrolled nursing.
2013	Alternative approach for trade positions	Alternative Pathways for the Trades Program announced to develop an alternative approach to the traditional trade apprenticeship model. Programme to trial an initial period of full-time training at a recognised training provider, followed by structured on-the-job training with an employer.
2014	Support measures	Announcement of Trade Support Loans of up to $20 000 over four years to apprentices undertaking a certificate III or IV qualification leading to occupations on the NSNL. Announcement of Australian Apprenticeship Support Network to replace Australian Apprenticeship Centres from 1 July 2015 with the aim to increase completion rates through targeted support to apprentices and employers.
2015	New South Wales	The New South Wales Government announced: $100 million will be invested to increase training options for employers, which will support over 46,000 training places for apprentices and trainees.
2015	Victoria	For the 2015-16 budget, Victorian Government announced: Back to Work Fund (a capped two year $100m fund) which includes $50m to help more Victorians start an apprenticeship of traineeship, from 1 July 2015. $3.5 million investment funding to continue support and guidance to apprentices aged 15-24 in their first year of apprenticeships for another 12 months (to 30 June 2016).
2015	Queensland	Queensland Government announced, from 1 July 2015: New payroll tax rebate to employers who hire new apprentices or trainees. $243 million for apprenticeships and trainees under User Choice. The programme supports up to 70 000 apprentices trainees across the state.
2015	Northern Territory	NT Government announced an additional $4.4 million for the 'Training for the Future - Employer Support Scheme (commenced July 2015). The Scheme will comprise of three grants for employers which are as follows: A commencement grant of $1000 paid when an apprenticeship/traineeship contract is recorded within the Department of Business apprenticeship database; A completion grant of $2000 paid when the apprentice or trainees training record has been classified as completed in the database; A recommencement grant of $500 paid to an employer who employs an apprentice or trainee at some other point during their training, e.g. an apprentice who leaves the employment of a previous employer
2016	Training	Apprenticeship Training - Alternative Delivery Pilots establish five industry-led pilots to trial the adoption of alternative approaches of delivering apprenticeship training outside of the traditional trade training models.
2016	Tasmania	Tasmanian government implemented a new grant programme ($600,000 in funding) called "Supporting Small Business with Apprenticeships and Traineeships Programme" to help small businesses to employ an apprentice or trainee. This programme will include assistance with obtaining business advice, support to recruit the right employee, planning the role of apprentice or trainee, mentoring and advice for the business and apprentice/trainee.
2016	Queensland	In Queensland, in addition to apprentice and trainee wages being exempt from payroll tax, employers can claim a 50% rebate for payroll taxes (previously it was 25%) for the 2016-7 and 2017-8 financial years
2017	New Skilling Australians Fund	The Australian Government announced, on 9 May 2017 in its 2017-18 budget, the new Skilling Australians Fund. The Government strengthened its commitment in the 2018-19 budget by guaranteeing a level of funding in addition to the revenue collected through the new Skilling Australians Fund (an estimated $1.5 billion over five years with matching funds from the states and territories). Also announced was a new $60 million Industry Specialist Mentoring for Australian Apprentices programme that will provide support to apprentices and trainees, particularly during their first two years, in order to improve retention rates.
2018	Industry Specialist Mentoring for Australian Apprenticeships	The Industry Specialist Mentoring for Australian Apprentices (ISMAA) program aims to increase apprentice retention rates, particularly in the first two years of training, in order to improve completion rates and support the supply of skilled workers in industries undergoing structural change.

Source: NCVER, 2018, VET Knowledge Bank Timeline of Australian VET policy initiatives 1998-2017.

A closer examination of recent patterns across states and territories indicate that the share of apprentices and trainees in-training has been declining since 2014. In the Australian Capital Territory, the percentage of apprentices in-training dropped by almost a half in 2016 compared to 2014, and has increased at a slow pace in the subsequent years (Figure 2.6). This share has dropped in all Australian states and territories, and can signal several possibilities, such as reduction in available apprenticeship opportunities, decline in interest among students, and increase in dropout rates.

Figure 2.6. The share of apprentices and trainees in Australia has been dropping

In-training, % of employed persons, across states and territories

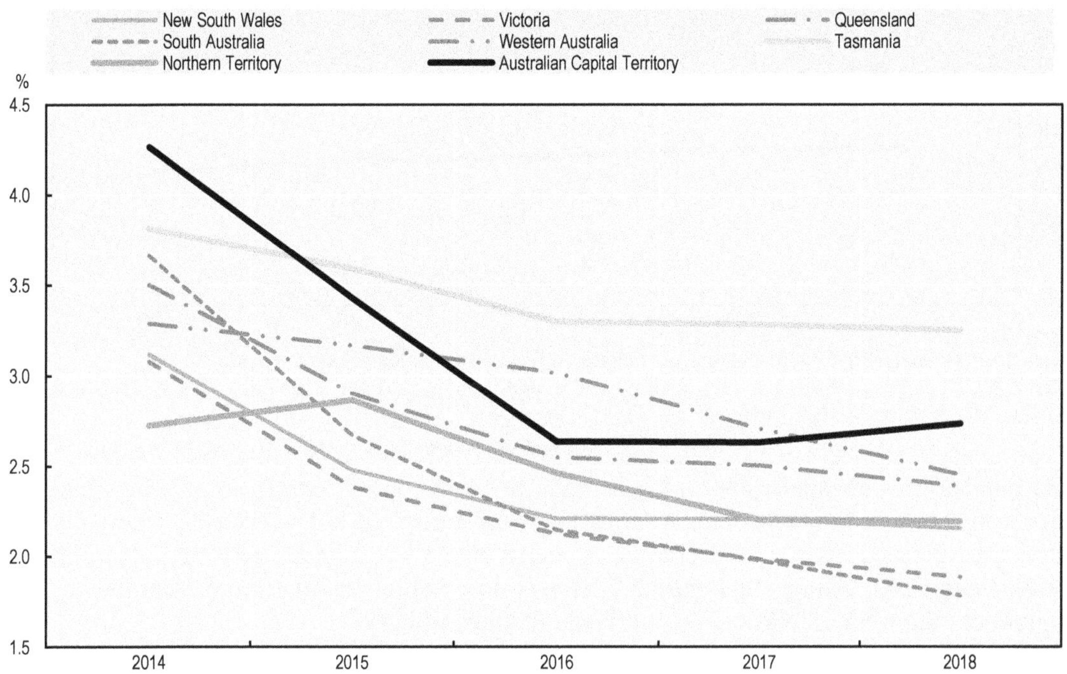

Note: Training rates are derived by calculating the number of apprentices and trainees (aged 15 years and over) in-training as at 31 March (NCVER data) as a percentage of employed persons (aged 15 years and over) as at February (ABS data). See ABS, Labour force, Australia, Detailed, Quarterly, June 2018, cat.no.6291.0.55.003.
Source: NCVER, 2018, Australian vocational education and training statistics: Data slicer: Apprentices and trainees, March 2018, NCVER, Adelaide.

StatLink https://doi.org/10.1787/888933932036

The number of apprentices in-training has slightly declined in both trade and non-trade positions across all states and territories between 2014 and 2018. The drop in non-trade positions was more pronounced than in trade positions (Figure 2.7, Figure 2.8). For non-trade positions, the drop was the greatest in New South Wales, where the number of apprentices in-training declined by around 25 000 units in 2018 compared to 2014, and in Victoria, where the number of people in-training more than halved over the same period (Figure 2.7). Australian Capital Territory, Northern Territory and Tasmania had the lowest number of apprentices in-training in non-trade positions but the numbers stayed stable in the recent years.

Figure 2.7. Number of Australians in-training, (non-trade occupations), by state and territory

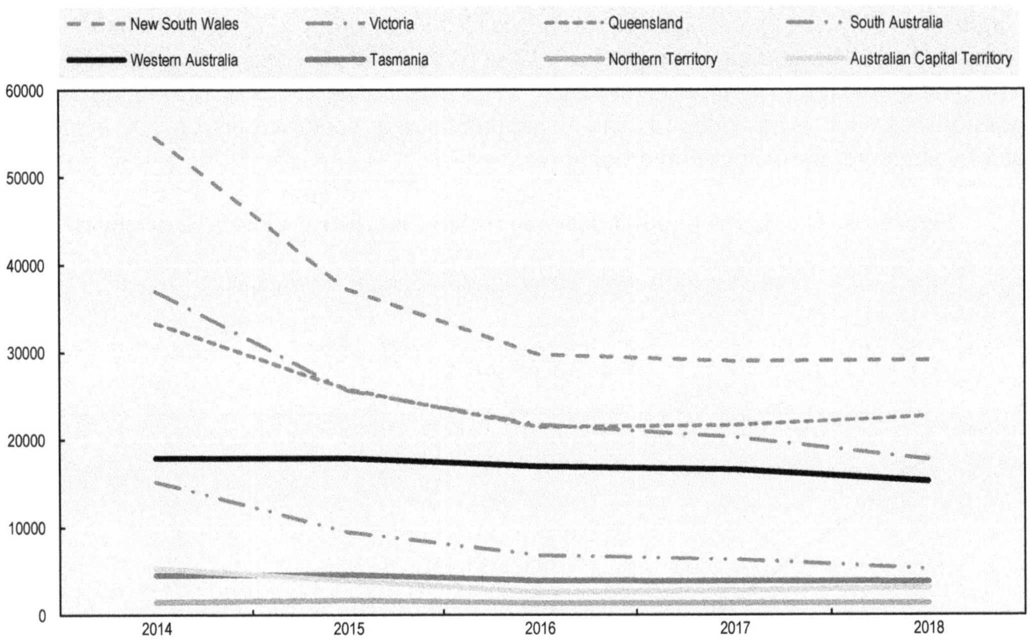

Note: As at 31 March 2018 for in-training. 12-months ending 31 March for all other statuses
Source: NCVER, 2018, Australian vocational education and training statistics: Data slicer: Apprentices and trainees, March 2018, NCVER, Adelaide.

StatLink https://doi.org/10.1787/888933932055

The number of Australians in-training in trade positions decreased across all states and territories, but to a limited extent. A large drop was registered in Queensland, where the number of persons in-training decreased by more than 10 000 unites between 2014 and 2018 (Figure 2.8). Similar to Figure 2.7, New South Wales has the largest number of apprentices in-training, followed by Victoria and Queensland.

Figure 2.8. Number of Australians in-training (trade occupations) by state and territory

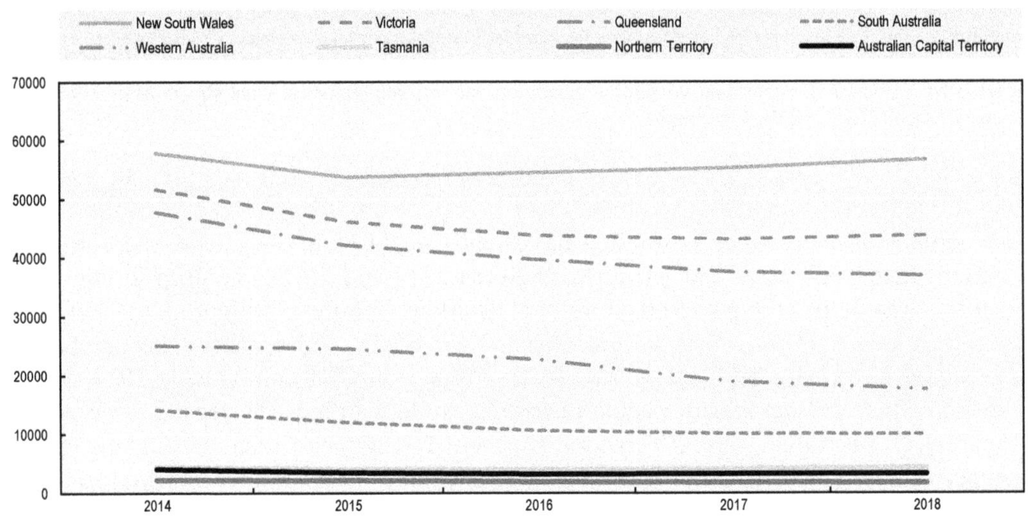

Note: As at 31 March 2018 for in-training. 12-months ending 31 March for all other statuses
Source: NCVER, 2018, Australian vocational education and training statistics: Data slicer: Apprentices and trainees, March 2018, NCVER, Adelaide.

StatLink https://doi.org/10.1787/888933932074

Figure 2.9 illustrates the long-term trend on the number of apprenticeship completions across states and territories from 1995. In 1995, the number of completions in 12 months was similar across most of the states and territories. As most of the apprentices are in New South Wales, Victoria, and Queensland, most of the completions come these states. The number of completions began to diverge from these three states compared to other states and territories throughout the period until 2012. Since then, these three states experienced a large drop in the number of completions, nearly by half.

Figure 2.9. Number of students completing apprenticeships or traineeships in 12 months (1995-2017)

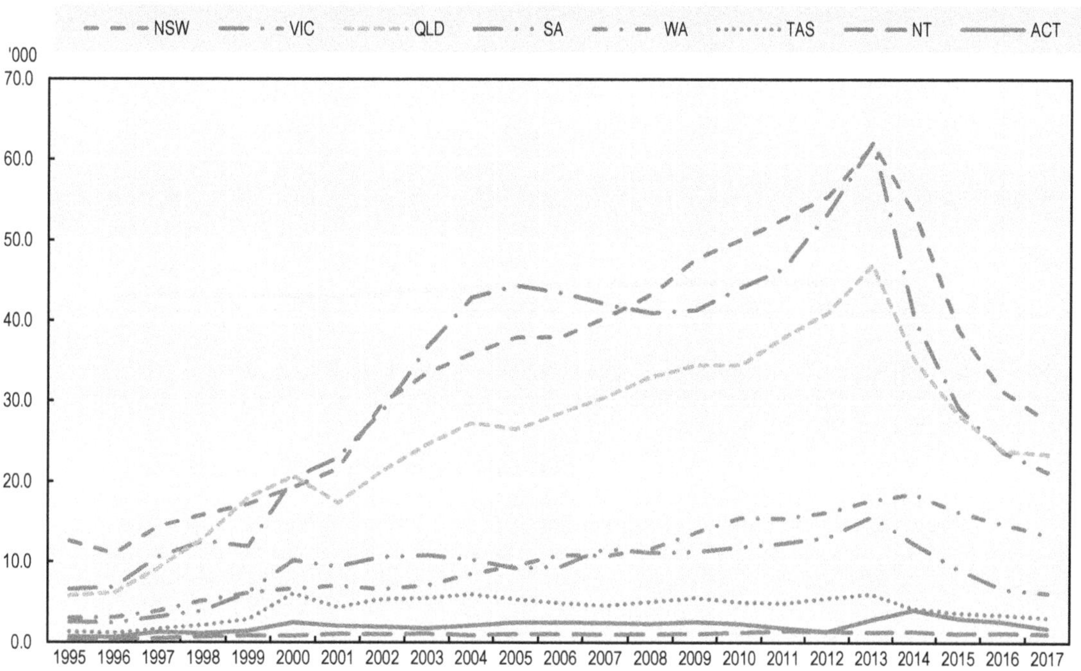

Source: NCVER, 2017, Historical time series of apprenticeships and traineeships in Australia, from 1963, NCVER, Adelaide.

StatLink https://doi.org/10.1787/888933932093

Similar to statistics on the percentage of students in-training, the number of completions in trade occupations decreased only slightly in the recent years whereas it dropped for non-trade occupations in New South Wales, Victoria, and Queensland (Figure 2.10, Figure 2.11).

Figure 2.10. The number of apprenticeship completions in non-trade occupations

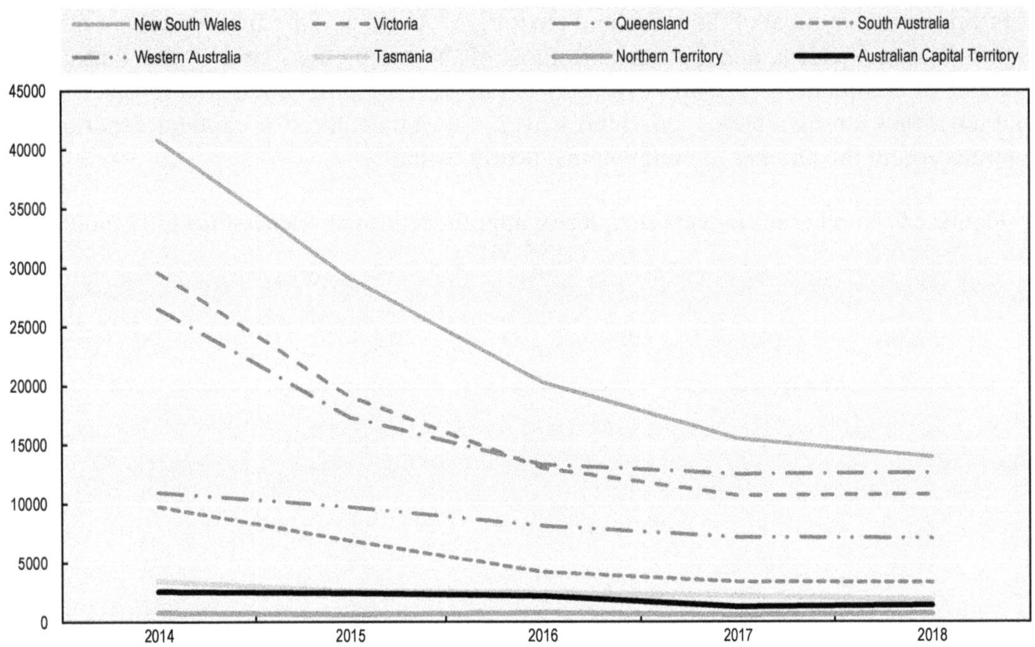

Note: As at 31 March 2018 for in-training. 12-months ending 31 March for all other statuses
Source: NCVER, 2018, Australian vocational education and training statistics: Data slicer: Apprentices and trainees, March 2018, NCVER, Adelaide.

StatLink https://doi.org/10.1787/888933932112

Figure 2.11. The number of apprenticeship completions in trade occupations

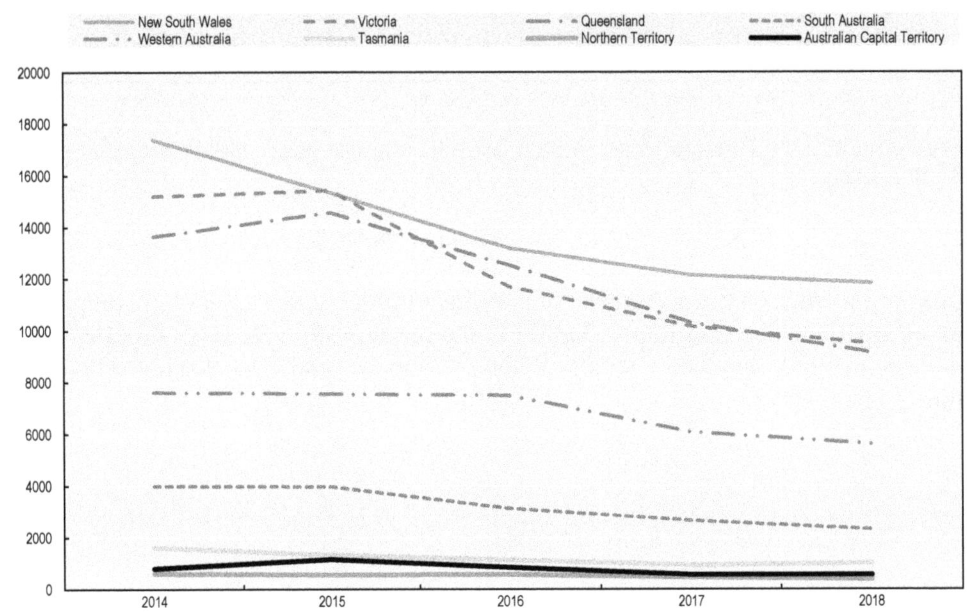

Note: As at 31 March 2018 for in-training. 12-months ending 31 March for all other statuses
Source: NCVER, 2018, Australian vocational education and training statistics: Data slicer: Apprentices and trainees, March 2018, NCVER, Adelaide.

StatLink https://doi.org/10.1787/888933932131

Another trend to consider is the number of cancellations and withdrawals from apprenticeship programmes. If the number of cancellations increase then accordingly the number of completions will drop and this can be exacerbated if the number of apprentices in-training is also decreasing. The number of cancellations and withdrawals in New South Wales, Victoria, and Queensland has been higher than other states and territories in the last few decades but in recent years, the number of cancellations has declined (Figure 2.12).

Figure 2.12. Number of apprenticeship cancellations/withdrawals in 12 months by state and territory

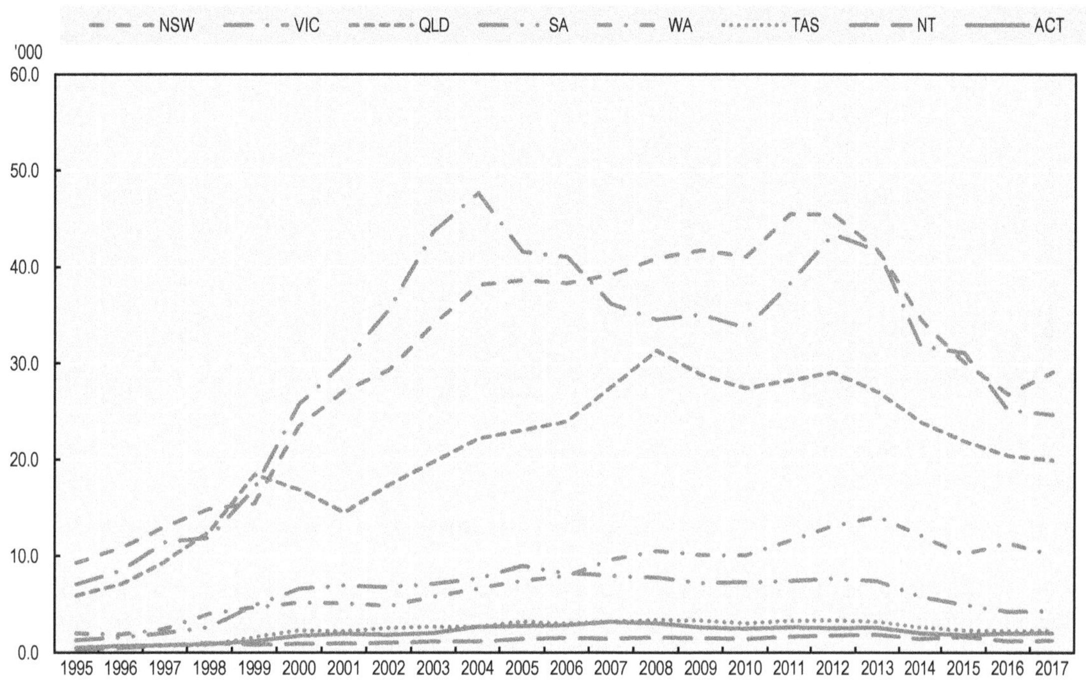

Source: NCVER, 2017, Historical time series of apprenticeships and traineeships in Australia, from 1963, NCVER, Adelaide.

StatLink https://doi.org/10.1787/888933932150

Within different trade occupations, the printing sector has the lowest and most stable number of cancellations (Figure 2.13). For all other trade occupations, this number has been increasing since the early 2000s. The largest number of cancellations is found among occupations in the building, other services, and metal and vehicle sectors. Furthermore, the number of cancellations in electrical positions rose three-fold compared to the early 2000s. Given that some of these sectors, such as electrical, metal and vehicle, face skill shortages in many Australian states and territories, more attention should be paid to reduce the number of cancellations and withdrawals in these sectors.

Figure 2.13. Number of apprenticeship cancellations/withdrawals by trade occupation

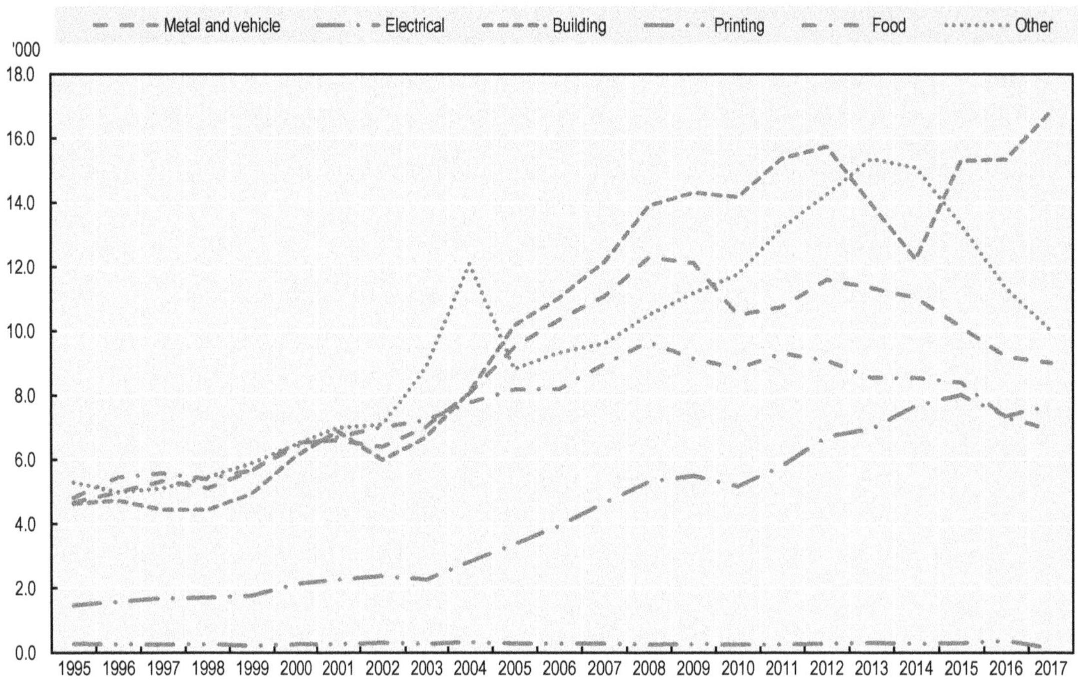

Source: NCVER, 2017, Historical time series of apprenticeships and traineeships in Australia, from 1963, NCVER, Adelaide.

StatLink https://doi.org/10.1787/888933932169

One of the outcomes to consider for VET is the share of students that did not have a job prior to training but found a job afterwards. Figure 2.14 indicates the percentage of students who are employed after completing a VET qualification (by all providers) by state and territory in 2017. The figures are derived from the National Student Outcomes Survey, which is an annual survey of students awarded a qualification (graduates), or who successfully complete part of a course and then leave the VET system (subject completers). For all states and territories, about one in two students found employment following the training. This share is the largest in the Northern Territory and Australian Capital Territory and the lowest in New South Wales. This is in line with earlier charts where New South Wales has the highest number for both apprenticeship cancellations and completions among Australian states and territories. Although this cannot paint a whole picture, it suggests that New South Wales can seek measures to improve training to better reflect the unmet needs and also efforts to recruit and retain more students in-training.

Figure 2.14. The percentage of students who were not employed before training but employed afterwards (2017)

By state and territory

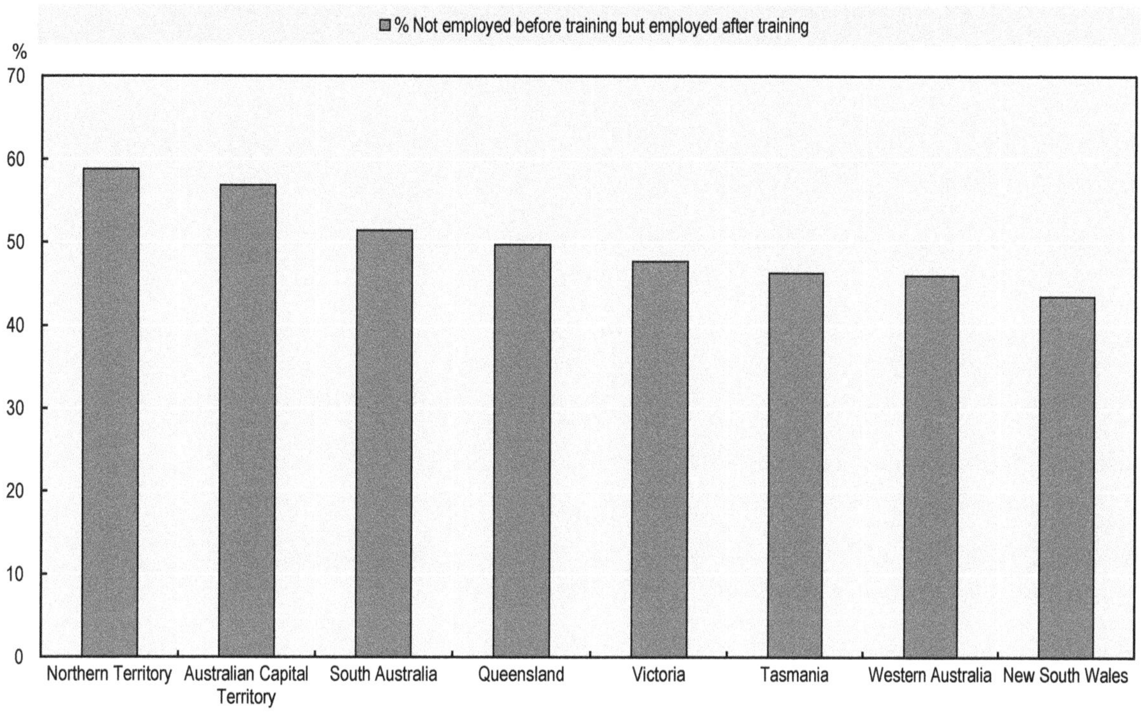

Source: NCVER, 2017, *VET student outcomes 2017*, NCVER, https://www.ncver.edu.au/research-and-statistics/publications/all-publications/vet-student-outcomes-2017.

StatLink https://doi.org/10.1787/888933932188

Notes

[1] In the Australian context, this classification includes all qualifications at Australian Qualifications Framework (AQF) Level 5 and above, i.e. Diploma (AQF 5) and Advanced Diploma (AQF 6), as well as Associate, Bachelor, Master's and Doctoral Degrees. Certificate-level qualifications are not included in this definition of tertiary education.

[2] An assessment of the performance of NSW ITABs has been undertaken on behalf of the NSW Department of Industry, and is available at: https://www.training.nsw.gov.au/forms_documents/itabs/itab_review_report_2016.pdf

References

Atkinson, G. and J. Stanwick (2016), *Trends in VET: policy and participation*, NCVER, Adelaide, https://www.ncver.edu.au/publications/publications/all-publications/trends-in-vet-policy-and-participation (accessed on 15 February 2018). [16]

Australian Bureau of Statistics (2013), *ANZSCO -- Australian and New Zealand Standard Classification of Occupations, 2013, Version 1.2*, http://www.abs.gov.au/ANZSCO. [24]

Australian Industry and Skills Committee (2017), *National training system*, https://www.aisc.net.au/content/national-training-system. [22]

Australian Industry and Skills Committee (2016), *Industry Reference Committees: Operating Framework for the Development of Training Packages*, https://www.aisc.net.au/sites/aisc/files/documents/operating-framework-201605.pdf. [21]

Australian Skills Quality Authority (2018), *Jurisdiction*, https://www.asqa.gov.au/about/agency-overview/jurisdiction. [20]

NCVER (2018), *Australian vocational education and training statistics: Data slicer: Apprentices and trainees, March 2018*, NCVER, Adelaide. [26]

NCVER (2018), *VET Knowledge Bank Timeline of Australian VET policy initiatives 1998-2017 | VOCEDplus, the international tertiary education and research database*, NCVER, Adelaide, http://www.voced.edu.au/vet-knowledge-bank-timeline-australian-vet-policy-initiatives-1998-2017 (accessed on 03 May 2018). [23]

NCVER (2017), *Historical time series of apprenticeships and traineeships in Australia, from 1963*, NCVER, Adelaide. [25]

NCVER (2017), *VET student outcomes 2017*, NCVER, Adelaide, https://www.ncver.edu.au/research-and-statistics/publications/all-publications/vet-student-outcomes-2017. [27]

OECD (2017), *Education at a Glance 2017: OECD Indicators*, OECD Publishing, Paris, http://dx.doi.org/10.1787/eag-2017-en. [15]

OECD (2014), *Education at a Glance 2014: OECD Indicators*, OECD Publishing, Paris, http://dx.doi.org/10.1787/eag-2014-en. [17]

OECD (2014), *Employment and Skills Strategies in Australia*, OECD Publishing, Paris, http://dx.doi.org/10.1787/9789264207899-en. [18]

Productivity Commission of the Australian Government (2018), *Report on Government Services 2018*, https://www.pc.gov.au/research/ongoing/report-on-government-services/2017/child-care-education-and-training/vocational-education-and-training. [19]

Chapter 3. OECD Skills Survey of Australian Employers

This section of the report presents findings from the OECD survey of Australian employers regarding apprenticeships. The results provide useful insights on the use of and the barriers to apprenticeships schemes. 95% of the 407 employers completing the survey were SMEs who have primary business operations catered to their local economic area.

OECD survey of Australian employers regarding skills and apprenticeships

Overview and characteristics of the respondents

In co-operation with the Australian Department of Education and Training, the OECD conducted an online survey among employers regarding their skills needs and evolving demands. A suitable sample was identified from the Australia Business Register database, and the survey was implemented from October to December 2017. Several multiple choice and closed-ended questions were asked as part of the survey, with the objective of better understanding employers' perspectives on skills development programmes.

While the results from the OECD survey cannot be generalised, they can still provide relevant insights on the use of and barriers to apprenticeships in key sectors, such as the construction sector.

This chapter will present the results based on 407 respondents (employers) who completed the entire survey. As shown in Table 3.1, the majority of the respondents come from South Australia and Western Australia, followed by Queensland, Tasmania and New South Wales. 95% of employers who completed the apprenticeship survey were small and medium enterprises (SMEs).

Table 3.1. Employers who completed the survey, by state and territory

State/territory	Number of employers	% of total
New South Wales	51	12.53
Victoria	43	10.57
Queensland	58	14.25
South Australia	76	18.67
Western Australia	65	15.97
Tasmania	53	13.02
Northern Territory	24	5.9
Australian Capital Territory	37	9.09
Total	407	100

Source: OECD Survey, Australia 2017

Figure 3.1. Distribution of firm sizes, response by the number of employees per firm

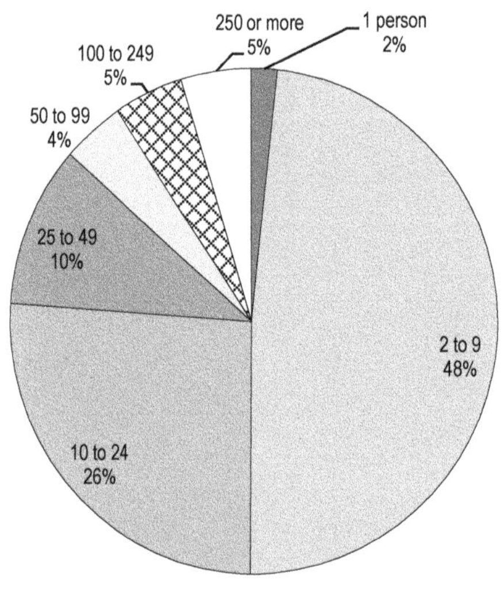

Source: OECD Survey, Australia 2017.

StatLink https://doi.org/10.1787/888933932207

The majority of the firms who participated in the survey were from the construction industry (132), followed by other services, manufacturing, electricity, water, and waste services (Table 3.2). There are very few employers in mining, wholesale trade, and administrative and support services who completed the survey.

Table 3.2. Most of the participating employers are from construction and service industries

Industry	Number of employers surveyed	% of total sample
Accommodation and Food Services	18	4.4
Administrative and support services	1	0.3
Agriculture, Forestry, Fishing	10	2.5
Arts and Recreation services	2	0.5
Construction	132	32.4
Education and training	16	3.9
Electricity, gas, water and waste services	27	6.6
Financial and insurance services	5	1.2
Health care and social assistance	9	2.2
Information media and telecommunication	2	0.5
Manufacturing	44	10.8
Mining	1	0.3
Other services	92	22.6
Professional, scientific and technical services	9	2.2
Public administration and safety	3	0.7
Rental, hiring and real estate services	2	0.5
Retail trade	25	6.1
Transport, Postal, and Warehousing	8	2.0
Wholesale trade	1	0.3
Total	407	100.0

Source: OECD Survey, Australia 2017.

Most of the employers surveyed had a similar number of employees in the past year. More than one in two employers in NSW responded that the number of employees in the company had increased compared to the previous year. This potentially points to a relatively stable employment situation among the employers who responded to the OECD survey. Given that nearly 50% of the employers who completed the survey are small in size (e.g. reporting 2-9 total employees) and that at least 80% employers reported that the firm size has remained the same or grew in the last year, this indicates that the survey mostly included firms that are not shrinking in size (Figure 3.2). This pattern holds true across most of the industries (Figure 3.3). About one in two employers in the construction sector reported growth in their company based on the number of workers in the past year. Most of the participating employers cater to a given local area or within the states (Figure 3.4). Except for 4% of the employers who cater to clients across the globe, the rest of the respondents cater towards local demands or within Australia.

Figure 3.2. Share of employers who had more, less, or similar number of employees in the past year

By Australian state and territory

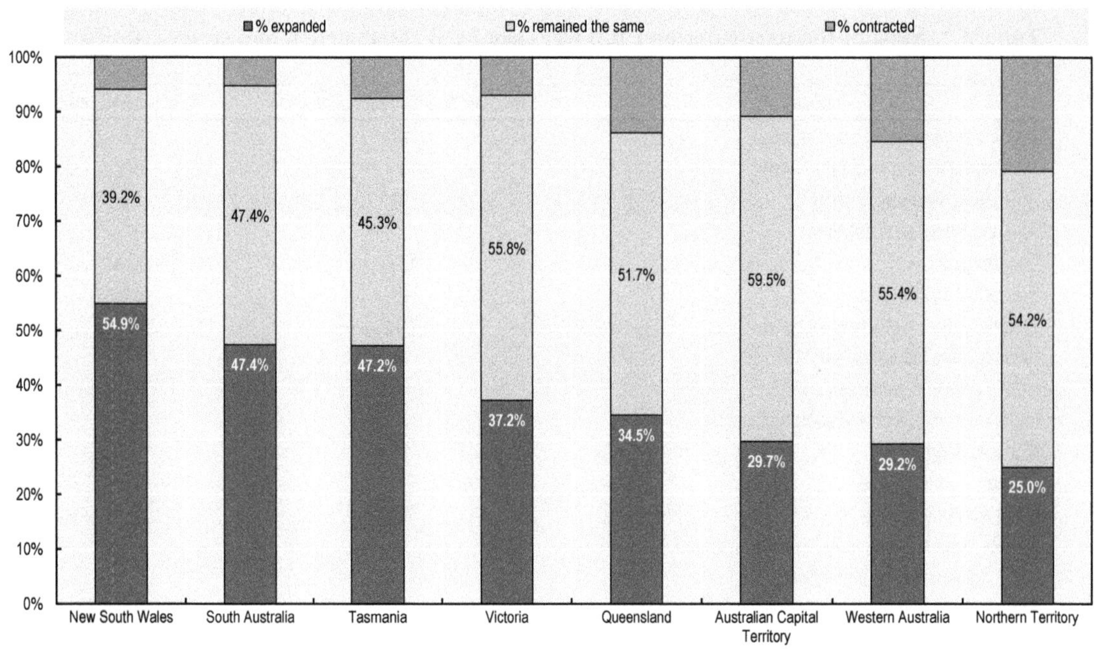

Source: OECD Survey, Australia 2017.

StatLink https://doi.org/10.1787/888933932226

Figure 3.3. Which employers experienced growth or reduction, by industry sector

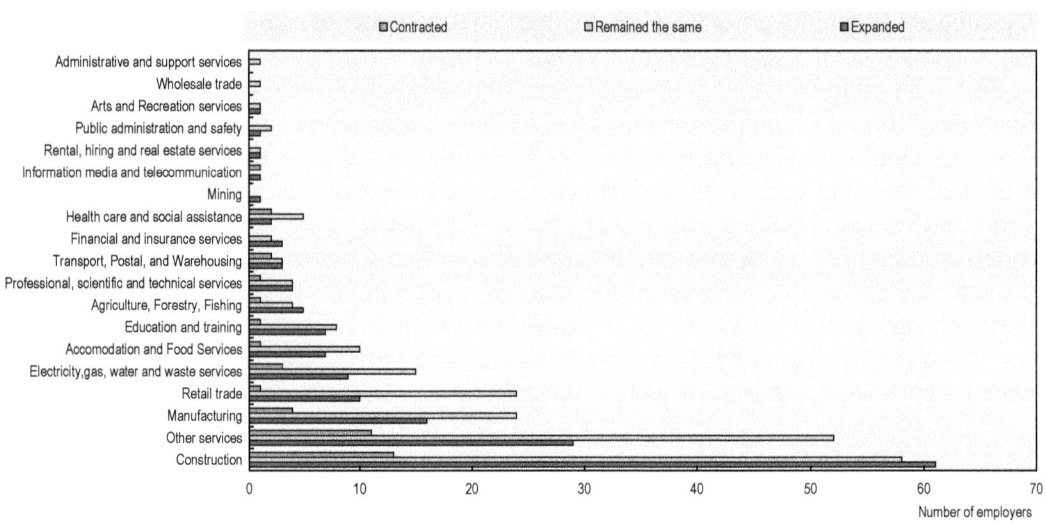

Source: OECD Survey, Australia 2017.

StatLink https://doi.org/10.1787/888933932245

Figure 3.4. Most of the employers cater to a given local or regional area

The share of employers that provide service or sell its products at the local, regional, or international level

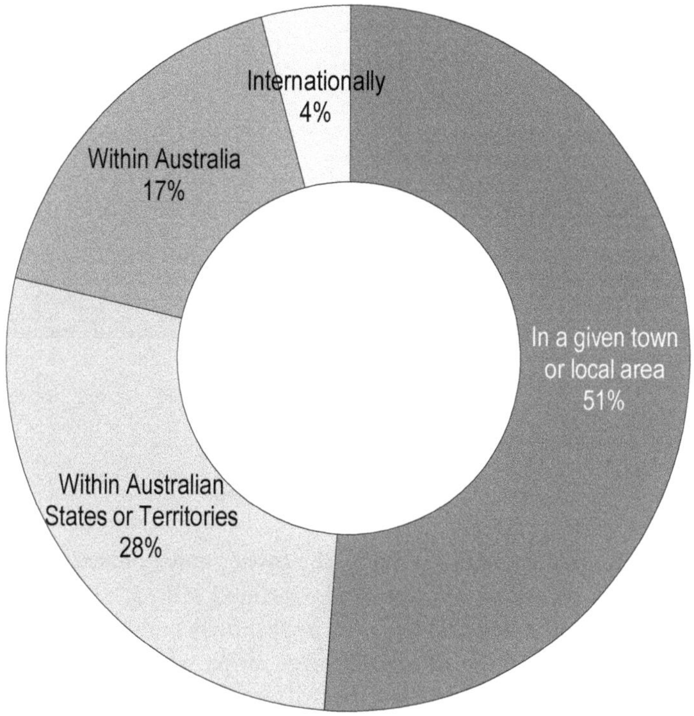

Source: OECD Survey, Australia 2017.

StatLink https://doi.org/10.1787/888933932264

Employers' perspectives on skills demand and apprenticeships

Figure 3.5 indicates that the majority of the surveyed employers are looking for advanced literacy and numeracy skills, followed by basic literacy skills, problem solving skills and advanced IT skills. Nearly 70% of the employers are looking for advanced literacy skills among apprentices. Some of the relatively less demanded skills include foreign language skills, social and emotional skills, technical skills specific to the job, management skills and manual skills specific to the job. Most of the employers chose advanced skills as important, rather than technical and manual skills that are specific to the positions. This can be partly explained by the fact that employers expect to train apprentices to develop these specific skills during their apprenticeship.

Figure 3.5. Skills that Australian employers are looking for among apprentices

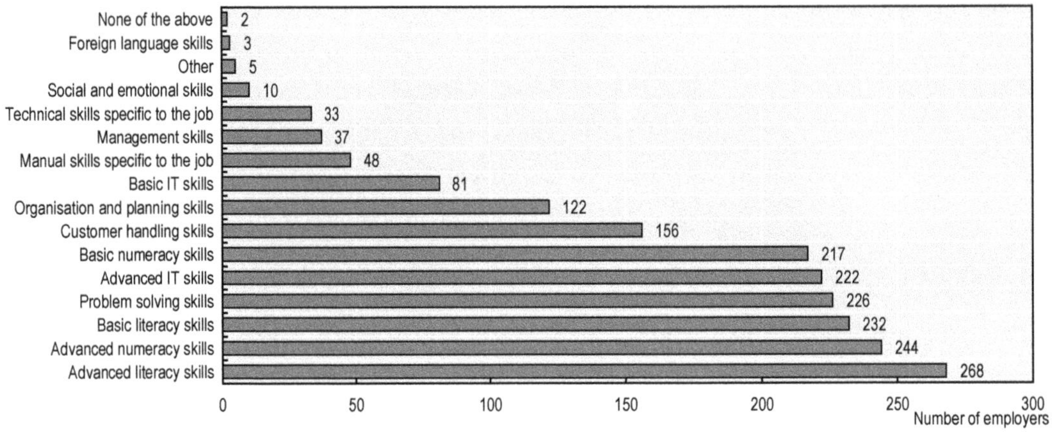

Source: OECD Survey, Australia 2017.

StatLink https://doi.org/10.1787/888933932283

As shown in Table 3.3, small businesses run by the owner may not have sufficient resources to offer apprenticeships regardless of their needs. Around 80% of small and medium-sized employers in the survey responded that they had apprentices in the past year. The likelihood of apprenticeship offers is the highest among large firms with more than 100 employees where 9 out of 10 employers responded that they offered apprenticeships. Large firms may have the capacity and the resources to systematically train and mentor the trainees as well as handle administrative tasks involved with offering apprenticeships.

Table 3.3. Share of employers who offered apprenticeship in the past year

By the size of firm/employer

Size of the firm/employer	Offered the apprenticeship	Did not offer the apprenticeship
1	14.3%	85.7%
2 to 9	77.7%	22.3%
10 to 24	88.7%	11.3%
25 to 49	88.1%	11.9%
50 to 99	70.6%	29.4%
100 to 249	89.5%	10.5%
250 or more	89.5%	10.5%

Source: OECD Survey, Australia 2017.

Figure 3.6 show that surveyed employers consider the lack of time and resources as the most common barrier for offering apprenticeship opportunities, despite government initiatives such as the Australian Apprenticeship Support network (AASN) and the Australian Apprenticeship Incentives Programme (AAIP). 21% of employers who completed the survey chose this as the reason for not offering apprenticeships. About a quarter of the employers also cited that apprentices lack either the skills (15.8%) or off-the-job training (7.9%) to meet the needs of the firm. 11.8% of the employers attributed having a past negative experience as a reason for not offering apprenticeships. Another 11.8% of the employers responded that having apprentices cost them too much and another 2.6% reported that they lacked the information in finding and taking on apprentices.

As shown from these responses, lacking relevant skills and high administrative burden and/or lack of resources for employers may lead to low apprenticeship opportunities and take up rates. There does not seem to be a huge variation across states in terms of apprenticeship opportunities. About 9 out of 10 employers in ACT (who participated in the survey) offered apprenticeships, followed by Northern Territory and Southern Australia. A quarter of employers in Western Australia, Victoria, and Tasmania did not offer apprenticeships.

Figure 3.6. Common reasons why employers do not offer apprenticeships

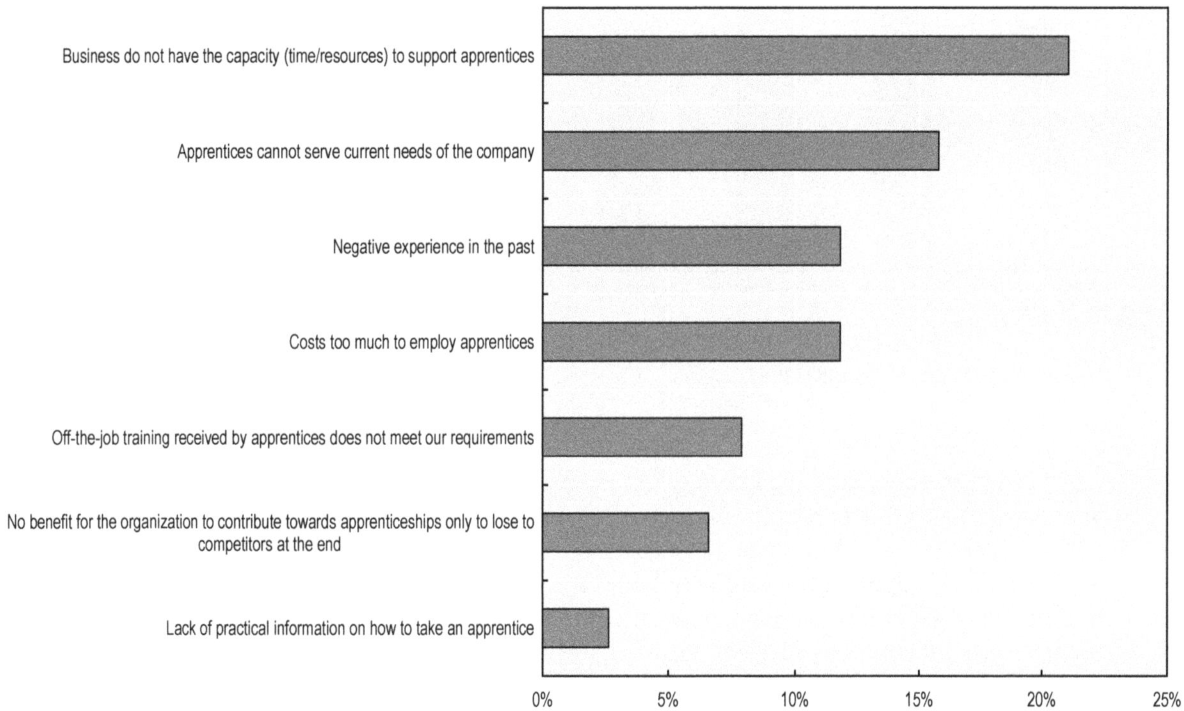

Source: OECD Survey, Australia 2017.

StatLink https://doi.org/10.1787/888933932302

Figure 3.7. Percentage of employers who offered apprenticeships by state and territory

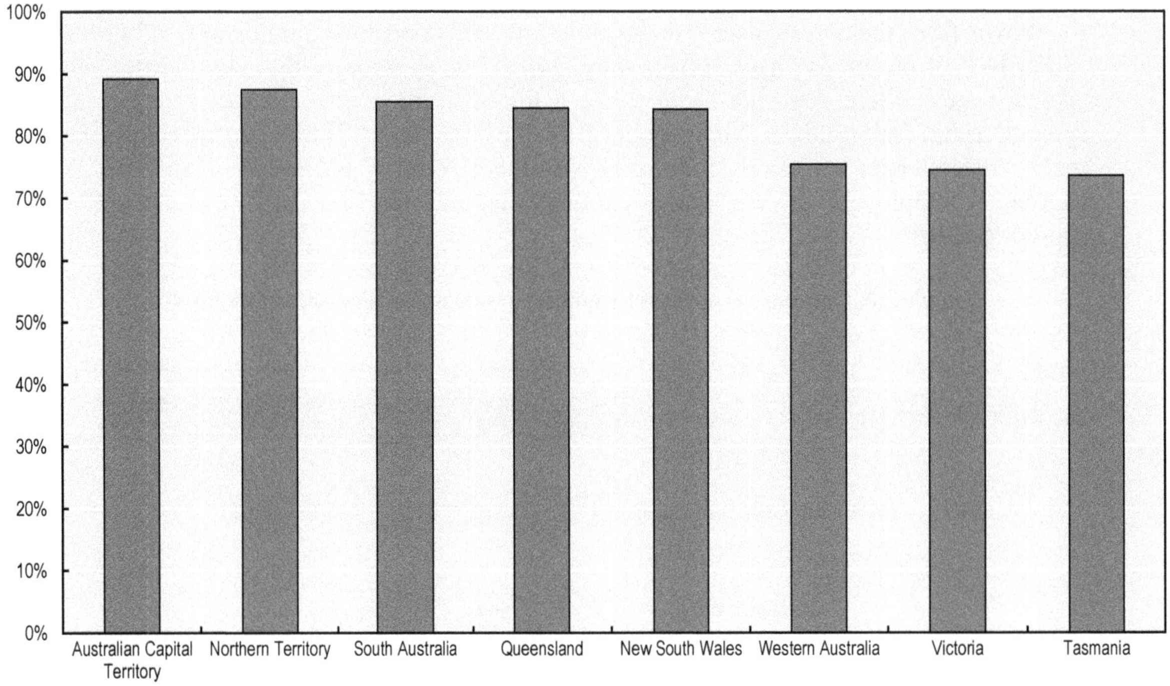

Source: OECD Survey, Australia 2017.

StatLink https://doi.org/10.1787/888933932321

All Australian employers who completed the survey offered apprenticeships in the past year across all sectors except for mining. The share of apprenticeships offered varies from 20% (Financial and insurance services) to 100% (Figure 3.8). This indicates that apprenticeship opportunities are available across various industries and sectors that traditionally did not have as many apprentices. The average number of apprentices hired in the past year ranges from 21 (Northern Territory) to 69 (South Australia). This is in line with the earlier figures where the Australian Capital Territory and Northern Territory have the lowest number of apprentices in training.

Figure 3.8. Which business offered apprenticeship in the past year

% within the industry sector survey respondents

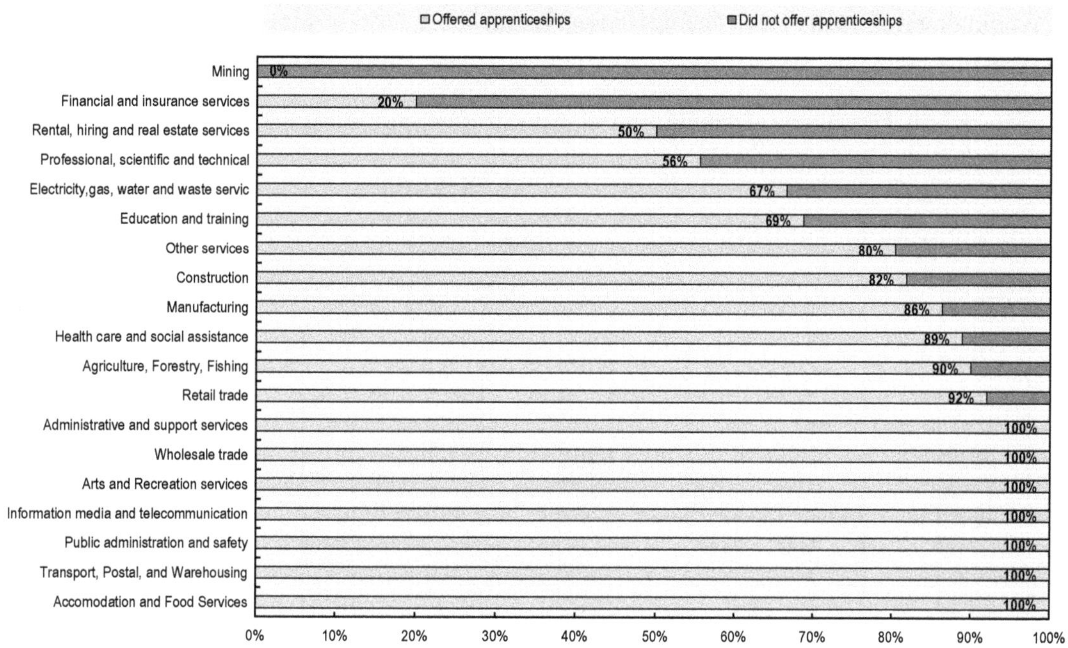

Source: OECD Survey, Australia 2017.

StatLink https://doi.org/10.1787/888933932340

Figure 3.9. Average number of apprentices employed by the firm in the past year

By Australian state and territory

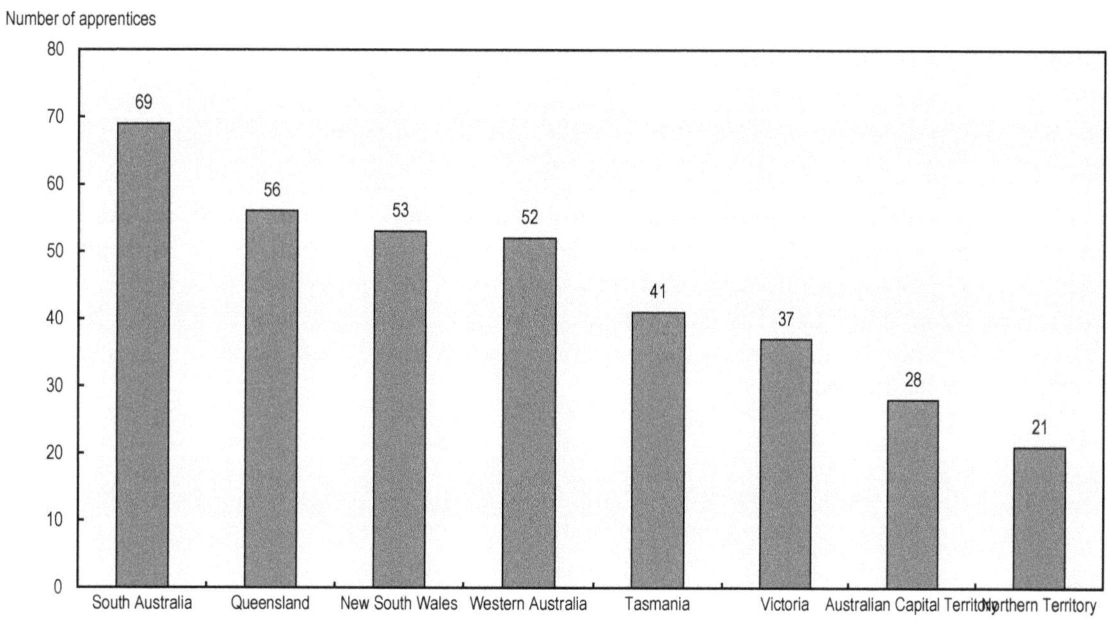

Source: OECD Survey, Australia 2017.

StatLink https://doi.org/10.1787/888933932359

At least one out of two employers surveyed in all Australian states and territories reported that they plan to offer the same or more number of apprenticeship opportunities in the future (Figure 3.10). In Victoria and New South Wales, two states that have the highest projected employment growth rate in the upcoming years, about 50% or higher share of employers responded that they would like to offer more apprenticeships than what they currently do.

Figure 3.10. Percentage of employers who plan to offer apprenticeship training in the future

By Australian state and territory

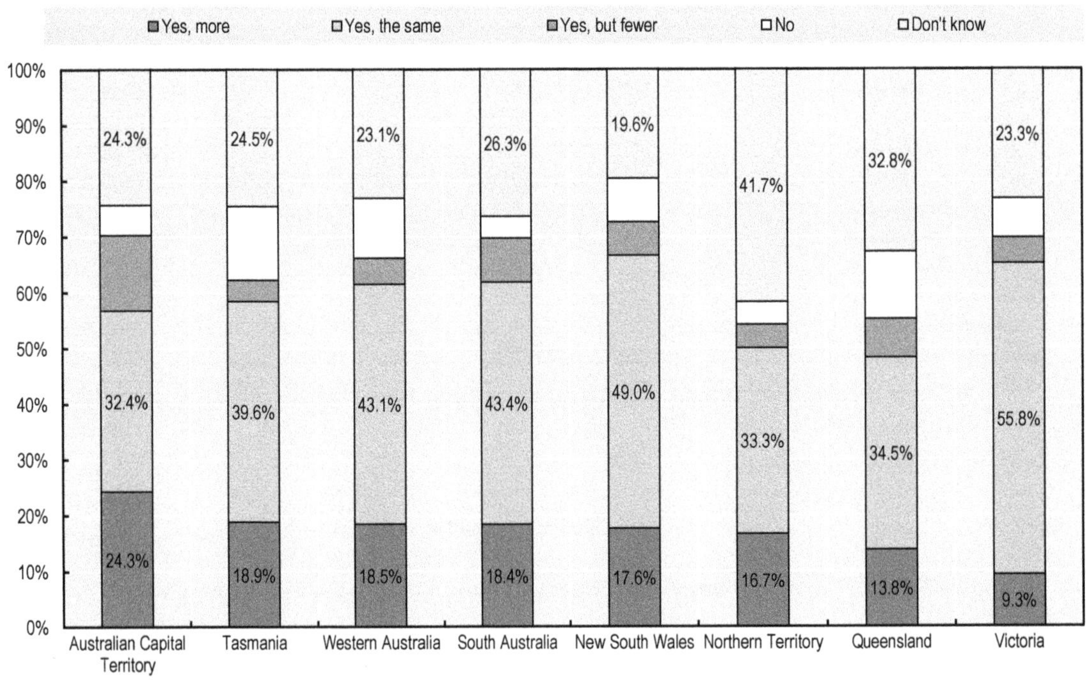

Source: OECD Survey, Australia 2017.

StatLink https://doi.org/10.1787/888933932378

The number of employers who responded that they usually keep apprentices on payroll once the apprenticeship is over ranges from 20 in Northern Territory to 65 in South Australia, for a total of 331 out of 407 surveyed employers (Figure 3.11). In South Australia, 32 employers responded that they keep 100% of the apprentices, which is a higher share than other states like Queensland and Western Australia. Overall, at least 50% of surveyed employers in all states and territories retain at least 75% of the apprentices on payroll when the training is done.

Figure 3.11. Percentage of apprentices who were retained after the apprenticeship

By Australian state and territory

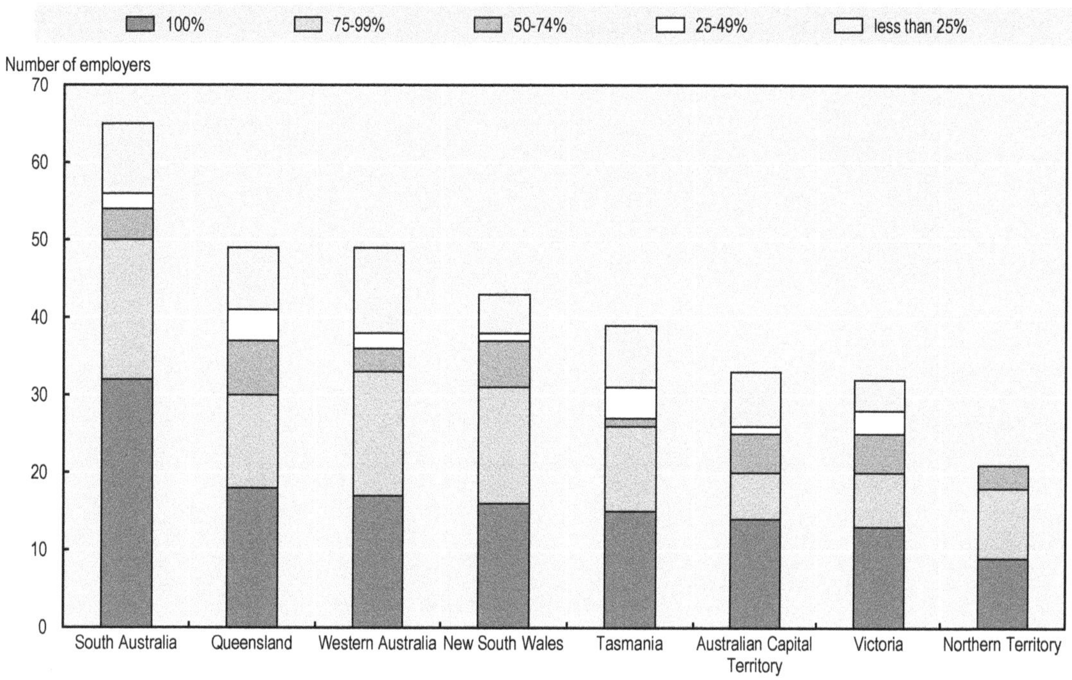

Source: OECD Survey, Australia 2017.

StatLink https://doi.org/10.1787/888933932397

Some industries are more likely to keep the apprentices than others. About 70% of the employers in the construction, manufacturing, and accommodation and food services industries reported that they keep at least 75% of the apprentices on payroll. On the other hand, Financial and insurance services, Public administration and safety, and Wholesale trade tend to have a higher share of employers reporting that they keep less than half of the apprentices (Figure 3.12). The retention rate of apprentices seems to be inversely correlated with firm size (Figure 3.13). 71 small sized firms (with 2 to 9 employees) reported that they kept 100% of the apprentices whereas less than 5 large sized firms (100 or more employees) reported doing so. This could suggest that SMEs benefit a lot from apprenticeship training and have high demand for apprentices and trainees.

Figure 3.12. Percentage of apprentices retained after the training, by business sector

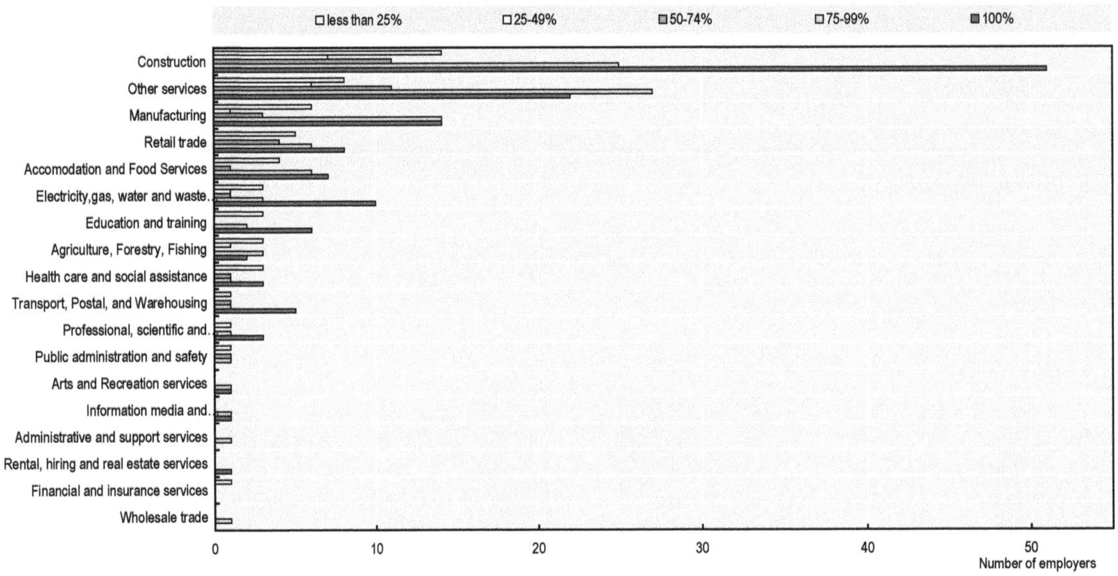

Source: OECD Survey, Australia 2017.

StatLink https://doi.org/10.1787/888933932416

Figure 3.13. The number of employers who retained all of the apprentices

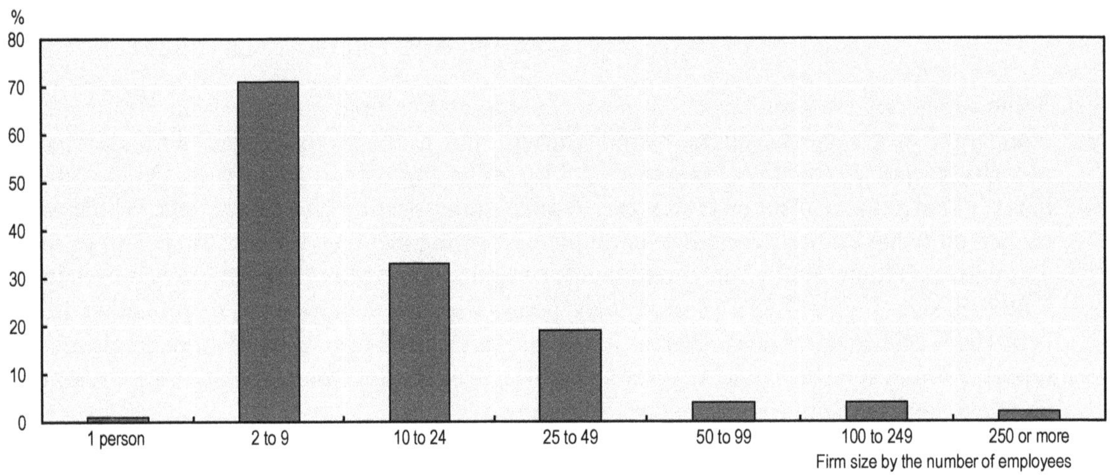

Source: OECD Survey, Australia 2017.

StatLink https://doi.org/10.1787/888933932435

When employers are asked to choose a maximum of three anticipated gains from having apprenticeship training, 70% of them responded that they try to maintain or improve future skill levels of their organisations (Figure 3.14). About 35% of the employers cited improved productivity levels and another 30% cited improved retention as a potential benefit from the apprenticeships. Improving the morale or image of the industry sector was not the top reason to have apprenticeship training from the employers' point of view.

Figure 3.14. What benefits do employers anticipate from apprenticeships?

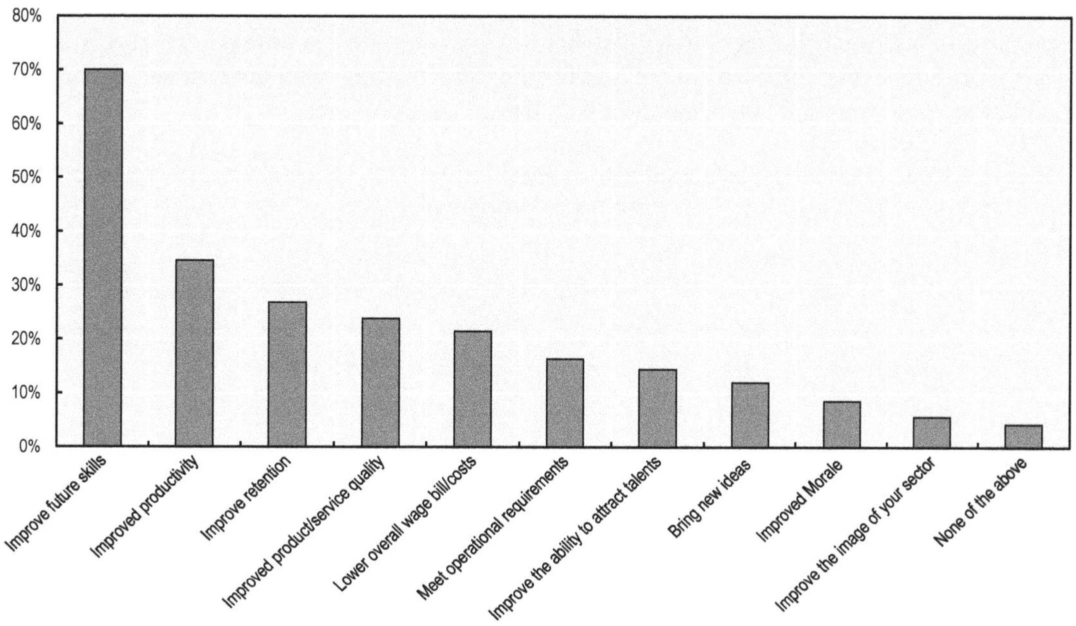

Source: OECD Survey, Australia 2017.

StatLink https://doi.org/10.1787/888933932454

On their main concerns about the current apprenticeship programme, nearly one quarter of the employers answered that they did not have any (Figure 3.15). The top commonly cited concerns about the current apprenticeship programme are poor collaboration with training organisations, inadequate off-the-job training by some of the apprentices and dropout. This suggests that training needs to be more aligned with industry demands and that stronger collaboration with the training sector is required.

Figure 3.15. Main concerns of the employers regarding the current apprenticeship programme

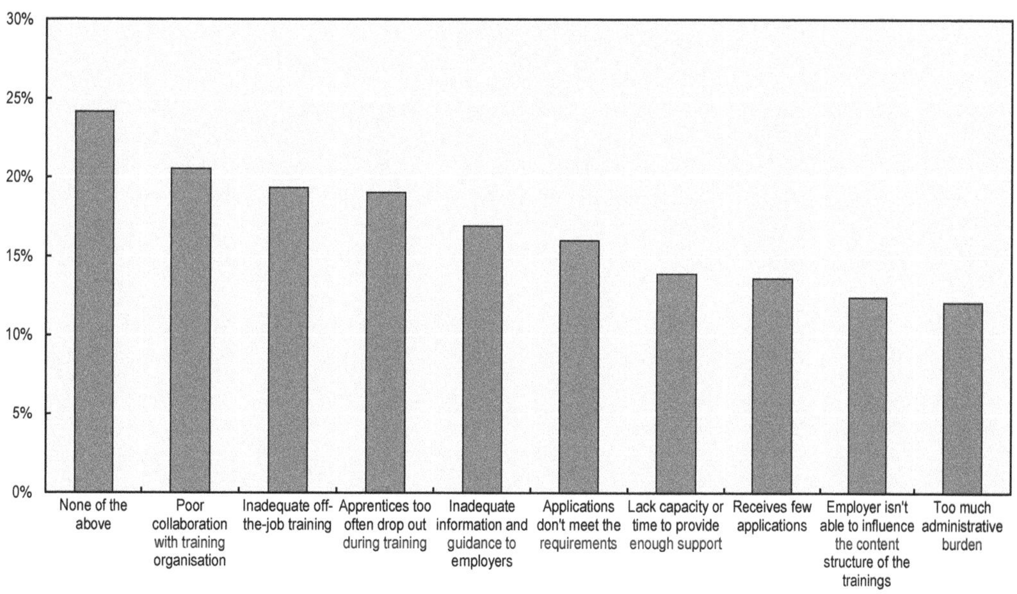

Source: OECD Survey, Australia 2017.

StatLink https://doi.org/10.1787/888933932473

Accordingly, many employers in the survey expressed strong interest in establishing partnerships with training providers for the design of training programmes. More than 250 employers indicated that they are somewhat or very interested in doing so (Figure 3.16). Also, the employers expressed interest in forming partnerships with government agencies and other employers but not as much as with the training providers.

Figure 3.16. Level of interests in establishing partnerships with stakeholders for the design of training programmes

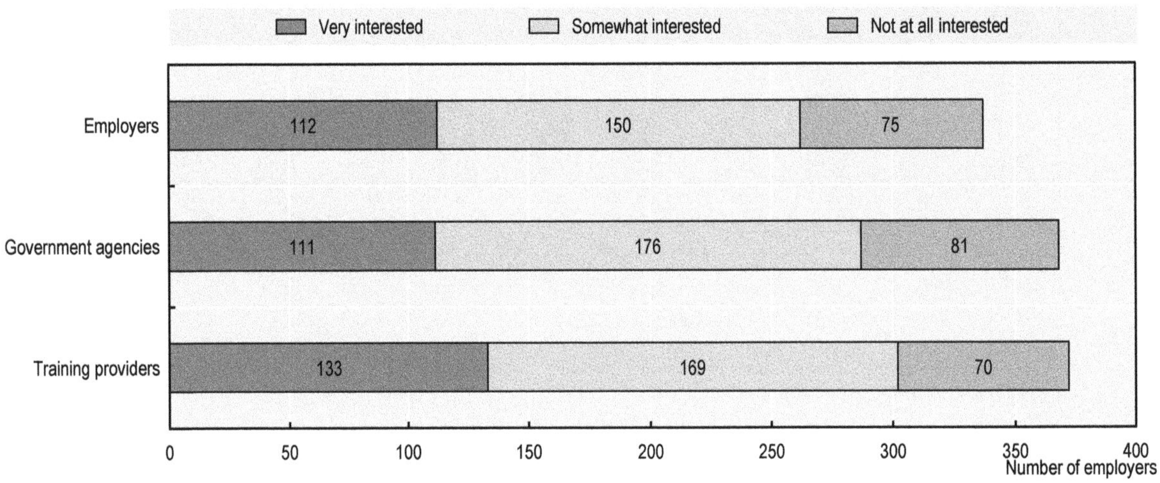

Source: OECD Survey, Australia 2017.

StatLink https://doi.org/10.1787/888933932492

Chapter 4. Taking a sector-based approach to workplace training – Sydney Metro Case Study

This chapter presents the first case study of this report looking at Sydney Metro, Australia's biggest public transport project. Sydney metro demonstrates the value of targeting apprenticeship programmes to sectors of the local economy. This case study also demonstrates the important co-ordination role that local leadership can take in bringing together key stakeholders to create tailored solutions to various skills and workforce development challenges.

Background

Sydney generates over 70% of New South Wales,' and more than one-fifth of Australia's gross output, competing with other international cities in the region such as Singapore and Hong Kong as a home for global investment (Infrastructure NSW, 2014[27]). The city is one of the most liveable cities in the world, with a population of 4.3 million expected to increase to 6.2 million by 2036 (Sydney Metro, 2016[28]). This growth means new transport infrastructure will be required to support the economy and Sydney's liveability.

In response to this anticipated demand, Sydney Metro is a key infrastructure project within New South Wales (NSW), and currently the largest public transport project in Australia, with over AUD 20 billion to be invested across the Northwest, Southwest and Central Sydney regions (Sydney Metro, 2017[29]; Sydney Metro, 2016[28]). So far, over 26 000 people have worked on the project that is scheduled to deliver Australia's first fully automated rail service, almost doubling the capacity of services entering the Sydney CBD (Sydney Metro, 2017[30]). Besides its scale and geographical spread, the project also has a long timeframe, Sydney Metro includes (Sydney Metro, 2017[29]; Sydney Metro, 2016[28]): 1) Sydney Metro Northwest, with a 2013-2019 delivery timeframe; 2) Sydney Metro City & Southwest - 2015-2024 delivery timeframe; and 3) The proposed Sydney Metro West (estimated timeframe of late 2020s).

Figure 4.1. Sydney Metro Project

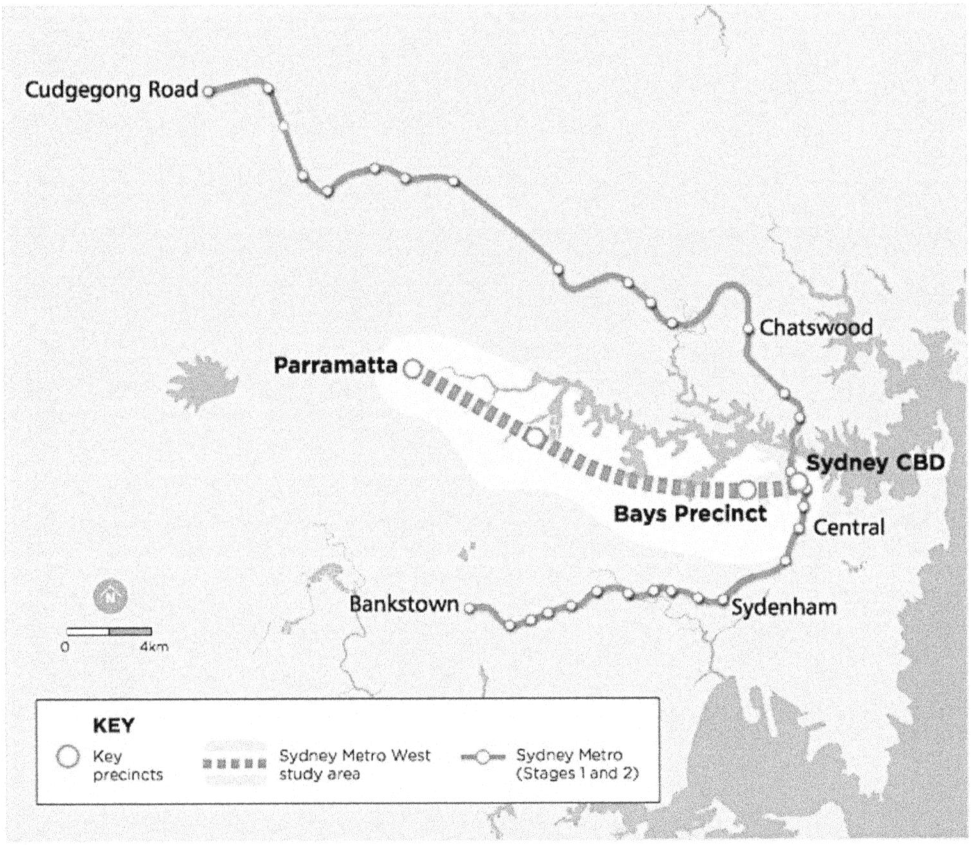

Source: Sydney Metro 2017

Key employment and skills challenges

Skill shortages in the region

Sydney Metro is being delivered at a time of unprecedented levels of infrastructure development in NSW and across Australia (Australian Bureau of Statistics, 2016[31]; Infrastructure NSW, 2014[27]; Wade, 2014[32]; Infrastructure Partnerships Australia, 2018[33]). The project involves extensive and complex tunnelling work and uses of state-of-the-art technology in construction and railing (Sydney Metro, 2017[34]). Delivering the project is challenging because a large proportion of workers in key industries do not have any formal training, and the workforce is ageing and lacks diversity, particularly in the rail and construction sectors. Furthermore, there is a reduced number of young people participating in VET programmes associated with the rail and construction sector.

Figure 4.2. Drivers of skill shortage affecting Sydney Metro delivery and operation

Note: Factors understood by Sydney Metro to drive skill shortage affecting their delivery and operation.
Source: Supplied by Author. Authors elaboration based on interviews with Sydney Metro.

Competing projects

To deliver the Sydney Metro project, there is a need for general civil construction workers and engineers. Many of the occupations featured in NSW's *skills shortage list* are of high priority for the project (e.g. construction estimators, surveyors, civil engineers professionals and technicians). This is happening at a time of unprecedented levels of competition for other infrastructure projects in NSW, where $49 billion worth of infrastructure investment is in the pipeline for transport projects and billions more for ports, airports, electricity generation, and other projects (Infrastructure Partnerships Australia, 2018[33]; Wade, 2014[32]). The resulting increased demand for skilled construction, engineering and transport/rail tradespeople, combined with other factors has led to skills shortages in construction trades, including carpenters and joiners, painting trade workers, fibrous plasterers, plumbers and cabinetmakers for the second consecutive year in 2016 (Australian Government, 2017[35]).

High proportion of low-skilled workers

In 2016, 31% of those employed in heavy/civil engineering, building and construction and 36% of those in rail transport did not have a technical qualification (i.e. their highest level of educational attainment was Year 12) and were not attending education/training (Australian Bureau of Statistics, 2016[31]). Employers in the construction sector have reported hiring unqualified but experienced applicants or final year apprentices due to their inability to recruit suitably qualified applicants (Australian Government, 2017[35]).

New technologies

In construction, key emerging technologies (e.g. use of computer applications, new materials and equipment, and artificial intelligence) that enable both complex construction work and provide potential improvements (such as remote operation and greater safety, mobility and precision) create new skills and training needs (Airbus Innovation, 2017[36]; Allen, Brasil and Manley, 2017[37]). In rail operations, the adoption of fully automated trains and other forms of autonomous operation translate into new workplace and job designs, which have new skills requirements. For example, being able to use communications technology and big data generated by wireless signalling and sensors for predictive monitoring and maintenance systems is now a key requirement (Australian Industry Standards, 2017[38]).

In addition to technical skills, there is increasing demand for employees with solid foundational skills, language, literacy and numeracy (LLN), and soft skills, such as communication and problem-solving, both in construction and rail. Being able to manage and communicate new safety standards is also becoming a priority as these industries embrace new technologies. The fact that a significant proportion of the workforce in these industries is formed by low-skilled workers, catering for higher skills level requirements means that not only will vocational training need to adapt, but also that significant efforts in terms of upskilling are needed (Pascutto, 2016[39]).

Low training uptake

Increased construction activity, combined with high numbers of low-skilled workers, and declining VET enrolments in the related sectors of engineering, building and information technology means the supply of qualified workers has been problematic (Australian Government, 2017[35]). This decline is also found across VET more broadly (Atkinson and Stanwick, 2016[40]). The number of suitable applicants per job vacancy in construction and engineering trades has been declining (Australian Government, 2017[35]), and research shows that approximately half of all apprenticeship contracts in the trade are not completed (Bednarz, 2014[41]; NCVER, 2016[42]). Part of the decline in VET uptake can be explained by the increased preference being given to higher education. There is a widespread perception amongst employers/industry that vocational education is seen as a second choice in Australia, discouraged by parents and not supported by career guidance provided in schools, especially for high performing students. Lower-performing students are three times more likely to follow a VET pathway (NCVER, 2013[43]).

Ageing workforce

Because of the decreasing uptake of vocational training, the ageing of the construction and transport/rail workforce becomes a problem. In the rail industry, for example, 52% of the workforce is aged over 45 (Australian Industry Standards, 2017[38]). There is a pressing need to expand the pool of qualified employees aged 25 and under to meet ongoing industry need for a qualified and talented workforce.

Lack of diversity

In Australia, women currently form 11% of people employed in heavy/civil engineering, building and construction, and 20% of those in rail transport (Australian Bureau of Statistics, 2018[44]). VET programme enrolments for 2017 show that men dominate VET qualifications in some fields. For instance, men represented around 90% of VET qualifications in both engineering and architecture and building, and almost 75% in information technology. While women currently form almost half of all VET students, and female enrolments have increased, they are concentrated in the health, education, personal services and management/commerce related qualifications (NCVER, 2018[45]).

Indigenous people are also underrepresented in heavy/civil engineering, building and construction and in rail transport across Australia – in 2016 they formed 2% of the workforce in these industries, while they were 3% of the working age population (Australian Bureau of Statistics, 2016[46]). This is in spite of the fact that Indigenous people were well represented (i.e. over 4%) in VET courses in IT, Building and Engineering in 2016 (NCVER, 2018[45]; Windley, 2017[47]).

To counterbalance the effects of increased demand and decreased supply of qualified workers and the need for higher-level skills posed by new technologies in the construction and rail industries, increasing uptake will require increased participation from groups that have traditionally been under-represented in these industries.

Unemployment

Youth unemployment and disengagement are also a problem that Sydney Metro is trying to tackle, particularly in Greater Western Sydney, where a major part of the project is being delivered. Western Sydney has had slightly higher youth unemployment rates compared to NSW in general. Most recently, the South West and Inner West Sydney had an average youth unemployment rate of 11.8% and 12.2% respectively, as compared to 10.3% for NSW over the 12 months from August 2017 to August 2018 (Australian Bureau of Statistics, 2018[44]). Some studies had shown that there are pockets where youth unemployment has been as high as 26% (O'Neill, 2017[48]). Young people living in Western Sydney are challenged by factors like poverty, lower education attainment, and concentration of industries with high risk of automation and change (e.g. hospitality and retail) – many who work, are employed on a casual or part-time basis (O'Neill, 2017[48]). Data also shows that youth disengagement was also higher in Western Sydney (7% in 2011, compared to 4% in the rest of Greater Sydney) (Australian Bureau of Statistics, 2017[49]). Another regional workforce related issue is long-term unemployment, which has been consistently higher in NSW compared to Australia as a whole (in 2016, the annual average of long-term unemployed people in NSW was 26%, compared with the Australian national figure of 24%) (Australian Bureau of Statistics, 2017[49]).

The development of a Sydney Metro workforce development strategy

Given the scale of Sydney Metro and the challenges described in the previous, workforce development was a key focus for Sydney Metro's delivery. When the project started six years ago, workforce development goals were presented as part of social sustainability commitments and were seen as a value-add generated by Sydney Metro. However, the new context of an increasing level of infrastructure development in NSW and rapid technological change has created the need for a more deliberate approach. As a result, the Sydney Metro Workforce Development Strategy has been a key element of the project's business case. To develop a strategy with appropriate priorities, objectives and measures/targets, Sydney Metro undertook extensive research and consultation with industry/employers, government, and the training sector, to gather intelligence around the (Sydney Metro, 2016[28]; Sydney Metro, 2017[30]):

- existing landscape in the construction and rail industries in terms of workforce supply and skills levels and what was needed going forward;
- current levels of training uptake, types of qualifications, quality of training design and delivery;
- existing NSW and Australian Government policy targets and legislative requirements for infrastructure projects related to job creation, business and workforce development, and the inclusion of diverse and disadvantaged groups;
- Underrepresented diversity and inclusion groups within the community.

The result of this intelligence work is a strategy that incorporates structured government, industry and training sector partnerships for the delivery of a highly skilled and transferable workforce.

Table 4.1. Sydney Metro Northwest workforce development target and actual outputs, in July 2018

Project Target		Actual to date
New Sustainable Jobs	622	1999
New Sustainable Jobs GWS (Number of the workers from Greater Western Sydney in Sustainable Jobs)	240	899
Apprentices/Trainees over 26 weeks	123	147
20% of the Workforce from Greater Western Sydney	560	1260
20% of the Workforce to participate in nationally recognised training	1426	3439
Diversity Target (overall target to employ workers in any of the following under-represented groups): • People with a (registered) disability • People from culturally and linguistically diverse backgrounds (CALD) • Young people under 25	2995	4694
Disadvantaged target (overall target to employ workers in any of the following under-represented groups): • Long term unemployed (over 26 weeks) • Young people not in education, employment or training (over 13 weeks) • Single parents of school age children	636	1108
Work experience placements, education placements, graduate placements (number of individual placements)	73	208
ANZ SMEs participating in the supply chain	360	369

Source: Data supplied by Sydney metro.

Figure 4.3. Sydney Metro workforce development strategic priorities

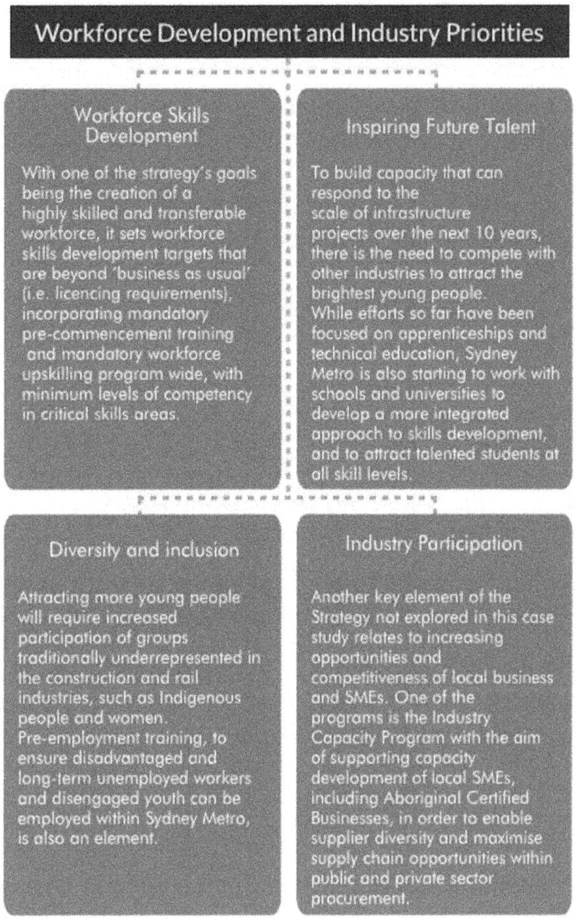

Source: Supplied by Author. Authors elaboration based on interviews with Sydney Metro

The approach to achieving outcomes linked to these priorities combines:

- Translation of strategic priorities into contractual requirements – contractors are required to deliver minimum workforce development and industry participation targets, and are given the opportunity, during the tendering phase, to propose methods and additional targets to suit their own project delivery.
- Industry and training sector engagement, with contractors and training providers working alongside state and national governments, to create partnerships around delivering targets, and also to gather intelligence to inform the strategy and its delivery.
- Developing flagship Sydney Metro led programs to bring stakeholders together, support contractors in the delivery of workforce development targets and achieve consistency across all contractors.
- Ensuring performance monitoring and management, to keep track of outcomes and of what contractors are delivering, and also to inform improvement and refinement of the strategy.

Using public procurement to deliver skills training

The main mechanism to deliver the Workforce Development and Industry Participation Strategy is to embed its targets into contract requirements and invite potential contractors to bid on particular targets. Contractors are expected to develop plans establishing how targets will be met through their project delivery, and are required to report on a regular basis about their performance against these targets. The Strategy is aligned with NSW state government policies to enable business, employment and entrepreneurship via its procurement directives (NSW Government, 2016[50]; NSW Government, 2017[51]). Minimum requirements include, but are not limited to:

- 20% of jobs are for the local workforce, with workers employed for a minimum of 26 weeks;
- 20% of the workforce must undertake upskilling accredited training. Training must be above business as usual standards to support workforce transferability and mitigate skill shortages/gaps;
- All workers in high risk occupations are required to undertake mandatory accredited pre-commencement training;
- Targets for apprentices and trainees working on site - minimum numbers will vary to suit the scope and scale of each contract package;
- Employment and training targets for under-represented groups, including Indigenous workers, women, young people, long-term unemployed, humanitarian programme entrants[1], and people from culturally and linguistically diverse backgrounds.

Development of partnerships through an advisory group

Sydney Metro identified that delivering the envisaged level of change would require the development of a strong industry-government-training partnership. In response, Sydney Metro initiated the creation of the Skills and Employment Advisory Group (SEAG) in 2014. SEAG was established in a strategic stakeholder forum model, which "is believed to be the only forum of its type, bringing together NSW and Australian governments, industry bodies, employers and training bodies" (Sydney Metro, 2017[30]). The SEAG and its members share an interest in Sydney Metro's workforce development objectives and provide a forum for feedback among local stakeholders. Together, their focus continues to be informing, advising and supporting the delivery of the Workforce Development Strategy and associated programmes by sharing current information and knowledge related to industry training and employment; assisting in identifying and addressing skills shortages and gaps based on skills profiles generated by each major contract; ffacilitating the conversation between industry/employers and the training sector; enabling the identification of key gaps and needs to be addressed in order to achieve the envisaged workforce development outcomes; assisting in identifying relevant funding sources; and promoting partnerships with government agencies (Sydney Metro, 2017[30]; Transport for NSW, 2017[52]).

The members, who are senior managers with decision-making responsibilities meet bi-monthly and represent Transport for NSW (Sydney Metro Delivery Office); NSW Department of Industry; Training Services NSW (State Training Authority); TAFE NSW; Australian Government Department of Education and Training; Australian Government Department of Jobs and Small Business; Sydney Metro Principal Contractors; PwC Skills for Australia ; and Australian Industry Standards. Other bodies are often invited to participate in discussions, such as local governments, representatives of other infrastructure projects, Jobactive providers, and diversity advocates.

Workforce development programmes introduced by Sydney Metro

Sydney Metro Industry Curriculum Program

Sydney Metro Industry Curriculum (SMIC) is a mandatory pre-commencement accredited training to meet minimum levels of competency for critical occupations within Sydney Metro. The objective is to establish new skills benchmarks, support the improvement of work health and safety, and increase the quality and productivity of the workforce. Critical skills areas identified so far are demolition; tunneling; general civil construction; rail; heavy haulage and leadership/supervisory skills across all industry disciplines (i.e. mandatory training for supervisors and team leaders).

Programs have been developed in partnership with registered training organisations (RTOs) to address Sydney Metro's needs, contractor requirements and scope of work. In addition, as part of the Aboriginal Participation Strategy, all workers at supervisory level are required to undertake cultural awareness training to build skills associated with successful engagement and retention of Indigenous employees.

Sydney Metro Upskilling Program

This program translates into targets that contractors are required to meet in terms of up-skilling a pre-determined percentage of their workforce throughout the life of the project. Training is contractor-led to ensure it meets both business and individual training needs, and must be accredited and extend beyond compliance/legislative-required training (e.g. licensing). During the bidding phase, contractors are invited to respond to this requirement by providing solutions that ensure new technologies are supported by new competency standards.

Sydney Metro Apprenticeship Program

Through SEAG, contractors expressed challenges in retaining an apprentice for the full apprenticeship due to the nature and duration of their specific projects. In response to this, the Sydney Metro Apprenticeship Program was developed with the collaboration of the lead Group Training Organisation (GTO) and launched in July 2017. Under this model, apprentices are hired by the GTO as a Sydney Metro apprentice, rather than being employed by a particular contractor, and rotate between contractors/projects as required. Contractors agree to host apprentices/trainees for an agreed period of time, as determined and facilitated by the GTO.

The model has a two-fold approach that ensures apprentices are able to complete their apprenticeship within Sydney Metro and contractors are able to meet or exceed their contractual targets (Sydney Metro, 2017[30]). The Program also provides mentoring and additional training and support as required, with the aim of reducing attrition. The expectation is that the Program will make Sydney Metro apprenticeships more attractive to high-performing students and, at the same time, support the inclusion of under-represented groups and increase workforce diversity. As of July 2018, the following has been reported:

- over 40 apprentices and trainees have participated in the programme
- 13% Aboriginal participation rate

- 23% female participation
- 60% of participants are under 25
- Retention rate currently at 90%

Pre-Employment Program

Through the research and consultations with major contractors, led by SEAG, it became apparent that often it was not the lack of technical skills that prohibited unemployed candidates from being employed, but the lack of soft skills such as communication, teamwork and problem-solving. As a result, the Pre-Employment Program was launched in November 2014, to equip long term unemployed candidates with key technical skills and the ability to communicate and work as part of a highly functioning team, with the involvement of potential employers in the training and mentoring process. One of the program's key approaches is 'team teaching', where language, literacy and numeracy specialist teachers work alongside students on the technical components of the course, with small group practical and assessment activities requiring participants to work collaboratively in order to successfully complete tasks. As of July 2018, Sydney Metro Pre-Employment Programs have been delivered with the following outcomes:

- 93 Participants
- 96% Successful completions
- 41% Aboriginal Participation
- 80% Participant employment outcomes
- 9% of participants through Prisoner Release Program

Infrastructure Skills Centres

Funded by both state and federal governments, three Infrastructure Skills Centres (Western, South West, and Inner Sydney) were launched in July 2017, to provide up to date infrastructure skills training, mentoring for apprentices and trainees, and to connect students to jobs. In collaboration with TAFE NSW, the centres host Sydney Metro workers undertaking pre-commencement training, along with those enrolled in the Pre-Employment Program.

The centres also aim to address skills and jobs requirements across other major construction projects, such as the Western Sydney Airport and WestConnex. It is expected that over 20 000 workers will receive training in the centres over the next five years. Integrated employment services, i.e. on site Jobactive providers, will advertise vacancies and link job seekers to jobs, within Sydney Metro. It is expected that training will be industry-led and co-designed, in a responsive and flexible way. Courses currently available include pre-employment and job-readiness programs; Sydney Metro Industry Curriculum; Work health and safety programs; Health and wellbeing; Technical, leadership and management training programs; Apprentice and traineeship support, and Aboriginal Participation programs.

Program outcomes

Given Sydney Metro's size and its strategic approach to workforce development, the project is creating new benchmarks and setting new expectations in workforce development for large-scale projects. Different elements of the strategy, such as the pre-employment program, and the advisory group (SEAG) have been recognised as best practices and replicated elsewhere both in NSW and other parts of Australia, including major projects such as WestConnex, Sydney Light Rail, and Capital Metro (Canberra), and in other sectors including hospitality, logistics, commercial cleaning and general construction.

The NSW Department of Industry has launched the Infrastructure Skills Legacy Program (ISLP), which builds on some of the training and employment requirements introduced by Sydney Metro (which is now a 'demonstration project' within the program). The aim of the ISLP is to capitalise on the record levels of infrastructure investment to increase the number of skilled construction workers and create pathways to employment across NSW.

Much of what is now part of the Workforce Development Strategy is the result of building trust, developing genuine partnerships and convincing stakeholders that having a shared approach to delivering the strategy produces gains not only for the project but also at a business level, through increased productivity and safety.

In terms of measureable outcomes, hundreds of employees have already benefited from Sydney Metro Workforce Development programs. Many workers with previously low levels of LLN (43% of the 2 400 SMIC participants) or no formal qualifications (55% of SMIC participants to date) have now received appropriate support and accredited training that meets Sydney Metro's quality standards. The Pre-Employment Program has also proven to be successful, with 80% of participants transitioning to employment.

Lessons learned

Sydney Metro's workforce development trajectory demonstrates that it takes time and effort to evolve from simply adding training targets to contracts into a more collaborative key stakeholder model, where stakeholders invest their own resources into the conception and development of tailored solutions. Some of the following challenges and key drivers of the outcomes achieved so far were highlighted by stakeholders from Sydney Metro.

Challenges faced during implementation

Establishing partnerships

Initially, collaboration within the SEAG between different government agencies (state and national) and between government and industry was challenging – government agencies were not used to collaborating in a systematic way, while industry partners saw each other as competitors and were not prepared to share information and practices. Sydney Metro took on the role of co-ordinating the group, and after months of meetings and working together around workforce development goals, Sydney Metro was able to convince stakeholders of the value of adopting a shared approach to deliver business level benefits.

Setting ambitious but feasible targets

From the project's inception, there was a clear intention of exceeding existing NSW Government requirements by integrating training and employment requirements into tender documents. However, this was not possible at first – commercial teams within government and industry partners both expressed concerns about the costs and risks imposed on contracts by including these obligations.

A case needed to be made to convince stakeholders of the business sense of this strategy. This was done by gathering evidence of the benefits of this approach from similar projects and getting leadership support. Sydney Metro now requires tenderers to include in any tender proposals their strategies for contributing to Sydney Metro's workforce development objectives, which means bidders now compete with each other to propose the best solutions. This is proving successful, not only because of the creative solutions being proposed but also because successful bidders have ownership of these solutions. It is expected that this will help to achieve outcomes, although this is yet to be measured.

Sydney Metro has also learnt from the first tendering round that contractual targets needed to be more specific and adapted to each type of contractor and project delivery phase. Initially, targets were quite broad (e.g. 15% of the workforce has to be formed by trainees/apprentices), when, depending on the specific work being contracted, this was sometimes beyond and other times below what a contractor could accommodate. The solution was to establish minimum requirements across the whole project with specific requirements for each contract package.

Drivers of success

Collaborative approach

From the project initiation stage, Sydney Metro investigated possible relationships with state and government agencies, employers and industry associations. Starting in 2013, the focus was on helping organisations involved in achieving their objectives, through Sydney Metro, to achieve mutual benefits. In early 2014, the SEAG was established to bring together all organisations and their expertise with the goal of achieving better outcomes. Initially there were difficulties as competing organisations and industry partners were unwilling to share information and practices. Later in 2014 this changed as industry competitors "realised the benefits of the shared approach and also increased their ability to engage directly with government and industry agencies" (Parry, 2017[53]).

Having a collaborative approach between governments, industry/employers and training sectors, via SEAG, ensures the strategy is appropriately tackling workforce issues experienced by employers, encouraging industry/employer buy-in. It is also appropriate for addressing workforce issues experienced across the whole of NSW and nationally. This collaborative approach also means that those government agencies which are more directly responsible for training and workforce development outcomes, but not directly responsible for delivering Sydney Metro, can support and drive Sydney Metro's workforce development programs. This was not always easy and industry partners had to be prepared to share information and practices within a framework that was built upon member trust.

Leadership from the client

Strong leadership from the client perspective (i.e. Transport for NSW) has meant that it has been possible to persist with the creation of partnerships, and also to ensure consistency – so critical for a project that is essentially being delivered through many different contract packages. Government leadership also facilitates the scalability and transferability of workforce development solutions.

Contractual obligations backed by flagship initiatives

Initiatives that specifically enable workforce development targets, such as the Apprenticeship Program and the Pre-Employment Program, has helped in achieving the workforce development contract requirements. Individual contractors will not necessarily know the most effective mechanisms and approaches to deliver the envisaged workforce development outcomes, but having these initiatives creates a simple avenue for employers to skill and support their workforce.

Note

[1] Australia's Humanitarian Program is the visa programme for refugees and others in refugee-like situations.

References

Airbus Innovation (2017), *IRC Skills Forecast and proposed Schedule of Work*, http://www.skillsimpact.com.au/skilliampactmedia/uploads/2017/05/ISF.FBP_.IRCSkillsForecast.2017-2020.pdf. [36]

Allen, R., N. Brasil and C. Manley (2017), *Future skills and training: A practical resource to help identify future skills and training*, https://www.aisc.net.au/sites/aisc/files/documents/Future%20Priority%20Skills%20Resource.pdf (accessed on 29 May 2018). [37]

Atkinson, G. and J. Stanwick (2016), *Trends in VET: policy and participation*, https://www.ncver.edu.au/__data/assets/pdf_file/0017/60722/Trends-in-VET.pdf (accessed on 1 June 2018). [40]

Australian Bureau of Statistics (2018), *SA4 - Summary Data, August 2018*, http://lmip.gov.au/default.aspx?LMIP/Downloads/ABSLabourForceRegion. [44]

Australian Bureau of Statistics (2017), *6291.0.55.001 - RM3 - Unemployed persons by Duration of job search and Labour market region (ASGS), July 1991 onwards.* [49]

Australian Bureau of Statistics (2016), *8762.0 Engineering Construction Activity, Australia.* [31]

Australian Bureau of Statistics (2016), *Indigenous Workforce Participation.* [46]

Australian Government (2017), *Labour Market Research - Construction Trades*, https://docs.jobs.gov.au/system/files/doc/other/ausconstructiontrades_3.pdf (accessed on 1 June 2018). [35]

Australian Industry Standards (2017), *Rail IRC skills forecast: key findings discussion paper 2017.* [38]

Bednarz, A. (2014), *Understanding the non-completion of apprentices*, https://www.ncver.edu.au/__data/assets/file/0016/9520/understanding-non-completion-2706.pdf. [41]

Infrastructure NSW (2014), *State Infrastructure Strategy Update 2014*, http://www.infrastructure.nsw.gov.au/media/1090/inf_j14_871_sis_report_book_web_new.pdf. [27]

Infrastructure Partnerships Australia (2018), *Australia & New Zealand Infrastructure Pipeline*, National Infrastructure Construction Schedule, https://infrastructurepipeline.org/. [33]

NCVER (2018), *SAS Visual Analystics Viewer*, https://va.ncver.edu.au/SASVisualAnalyticsViewer/VisualAnalyticsViewer_guest.jsp?reportName=VET%20students%20by%20industry&reportPath=/Visual%20Analytics/NCVER/vpc-total-vet-activity/Reports/3.Published&appSwitcherDisabled=true&commentsEnabled=false&repor. [45]

NCVER (2016), *Apprentices and trainees 2016: infographic*, http://www.voced.edu.au/content/ngv%3A77283. [42]

NCVER (2013), *Youth transitions in Australia: a moving picture*, https://www.ncver.edu.au/__data/assets/file/0026/46349/youth-transitions-in-aus-2772.pdf (accessed on 29 May 2018). [43]

NSW Government (2017), *PBD-2017-05 Construction training and skills development*, https://arp.nsw.gov.au/pbd-2017-05-construction-training-and-skills-development. [51]

NSW Government (2016), *Aboriginal Participation in Construction*, https://www.procurepoint.nsw.gov.au/system/files/documents/apic_policy_1_august_2016.pdf (accessed on 1 June 2018). [50]

O'Neill, P. (2017), *Youth Unemployment in Western Sydney*, Centre for Western Sydney, https://www.westernsydney.edu.au/__data/assets/pdf_file/0010/1269064/YA_unemployment_fnl_V6.1.pdf. [48]

Parry, C. (2017), *Consultation with Sydney Metro*. [53]

Pascutto, N. (2016), *CROSSRAIL SKILLS & EMPLOYMENT STRATEGY*. [39]

Sydney Metro (2017), *Industry briefing November 2017*, https://www.sydneymetro.info/sites/default/files/Sydney%20Metro%20Industry%20Briefing%20PowerPoint%20November%202017.pdf. [34]

Sydney Metro (2017), *Industry Briefing, April 2017*. [29]

Sydney Metro (2017), *Workforce development and industry participation strategy 2016-2019 [DRAFT]*. [30]

Sydney Metro (2016), *Final Business Case*, https://www.sydneymetro.info/sites/default/files/Sydney%20Metro%20CSW%20Business%20Case%20Summary.pdf. [28]

Transport for NSW (2017), *Sydney Metro Skills and Employment Advisory Group (SEAG) Terms of Reference*. [52]

Wade, M. (2014), *NSW seen as world's infrastructure capital thanks to $85b in projects, says Mike Baird*, https://www.smh.com.au/national/nsw/nsw-seen-as-worlds-infrastructure-capital-thanks-to-85b-in-projects-says-mike-baird-20140202-31v07.html. [32]

Windley, G. (2017), *Indigenous VET participation, completion and outcomes: change over the past decade*, https://www.ncver.edu.au/__data/assets/pdf_file/0031/484447/Indigenous-VET-participation,-completion-and-outcomes.pdf.. [47]

Chapter 5. Moving a local economy to higher value added skills – STEMship Case Study

The following case study, based in a major regional centre in New South Wales, demonstrates how partnerships between local community, industry and training sectors can deliver a multi-disciplinary approach to vocational education and training to equip individuals with digital literacy skills in emerging STEM occupations.

Background

STEMship is Australia's first vocational education and training pre-employment programme focusing on the development of STEM skills at a technical level and the creation of a highly skilled pool of talent (STEMship, 2017[54]). The programme was developed by Regional Development Australia (RDA Hunter) and the NSW Department of Industry (Training Services NSW), and delivered by TAFE NSW. Pivotal to the programme's design is an industry-led approach, which provides a VET pathway for students to move into employment, highly technical apprenticeships and traineeships, higher-level Certificate IV, Diploma qualifications, or University.

Skills for a knowledge economy

The Hunter Region is Australia's largest regional area, hosting Australia's seventh largest city, Newcastle. It is also Australia's largest and most diverse regional economy, with an output of AUD 41 million in 2017 (equivalent of 3% of Australia's), generated by a diverse range of industries, including services (71% of the region's output), mineral resources (11%), manufacturing (9%), construction (7%), and agriculture (2%) (Australian Bureau of Statistics, 2016[55]; Australian Government Department of Jobs and Small Business, 2018[56]).

During the last two decades, employment in the Hunter Valley region (excluding Newcastle) has moved away from manufacturing and agriculture, to services (with the largest increase in employment recorded over almost the last 20 years recorded in the Health Care and Social Assistance industry, followed by Mining, Construction and Professional, Scientific and Technical Services) (Australian Bureau of Statistics, 2018[57]). Almost half of Australian start-ups are located in NSW, and Newcastle intends to increase its share of this market and becoming a hub for start-up business (Startup Muster, 2015[58]).

This means the local economy is becoming more and more knowledge oriented, and will increasingly rely on the development of higher-level skills to support growth through increased competitiveness. Local leadership, through RDA Hunter, is aware of this challenge, and has encouraged and facilitated industry engagement in skills development through a range of initiatives, including the Hunter Innovation Scorecard, Hunter Innovation Festivals, the ME Programme and the Business Innovation Hub.

Challenges within the current VET system

As part of their workforce development strategy, RDA Hunter has been facilitating partnerships between industry and the education and training system for the development of STEM skills since 2009. Initially, the focus was on secondary education, but industry partners expressed the need for a more specific focus on technical education. For many of the available STEM-related roles, industry partners prefer to recruit employees with technical skills and industry experience rather than academic knowledge.

This demand for a technical STEM workforce is consistent across Australia. Between 2006-11, jobs requiring STEM skills grew about 1.5 times the rate of other jobs (Australian Bureau of Statistics, 2015[59]). However, finding an appropriately skilled workforce has proven somewhat difficult. In a survey of employers undertaken on behalf of the Australian Government (2013), 40% of respondents reported difficulty in recruiting STEM-skilled technician and trades workers. While 20% of employers reported a shortage of graduates, around a third reported a mismatch between the skills required and those of job applicants (Prinsley and Baranyai, 2015[60]).

In the same survey, while over two thirds of responding employers thought relevant work experience was an important candidate attribute for STEM roles, only around a third of respondents were offering structured work placements to applicable students. Employers indicated dissatisfaction with post-secondary education institutions (just over 50% were actually satisfied with their experience). Concerns regarding the poor level of industry engagement to develop business relevant STEM courses were highlighted.

Need for multi-disciplinary approach

Regular pre-apprenticeship programmes direct students towards a specific occupation, which traditionally tend to be associated with particular industries. For example, if a student is engaged in a pre-apprenticeship programme in Carpentry and Joinery, they will complete almost half of the core units of competency of a full Carpentry and Joinery apprenticeship over a total period of 15 weeks.

One of the issues with this model is that there is not a focus on the development of multidisciplinary skills. Local employers are clear that emerging technologies, markets and new ways of working, mean the roles they need to fill increasingly involve a broad spectrum of expertise. For example, in engineering fabrication, workers need to be able to deal with heavy and light fabrication, understand design principles, and how the business works in a management and marketing sense.

Consultations undertaken by RDA Hunter also suggest that potential employees are more attractive when they have well-developed digital literacy and soft skills (e.g. communication, team working, complex problem solving, creativity and innovation). Even though the current VET system is designed to enable a degree of skills transferability, through the development of a set of core 'employability skills', it does not do so in a multidisciplinary way; these skills are developed within qualifications in occupation-specific ways, limiting their transferability (Snell, Gerkara and Gatt, 2016[61]).

Technological, economic and societal trends are pushing towards the need to focus training on skills rather than occupations/jobs, so that skills are applicable to multiple workplace contexts and industries. Studies stimulating this discussion are gaining traction in Australia (Allen, Brasil and Manley, 2017[62]; Foundation for Young Australians, 2017[63]).

Another issue with the current model is that, because industry normally does not have much control over training plans (meaning that training is not necessarily relevant and/or students can leave pre-apprenticeship programmes with little industry understanding/experience), students completing pre-apprenticeship programmes, who would have a considerable portion of their apprenticeship certificate already completed (therefore entitled to be hired with the wage of a 2nd year apprentice), could be less attractive/competitive than someone with less qualification.

Programme approach

STEMship is a pre-employment programme, offering a multidisciplinary VET pathway for secondary school graduates to enter highly technical apprenticeships and traineeships as an alternative to direct entry to University. The programme was developed in 2016 by RDA Hunter which co-ordinates the programme through extensive consultation with local industries, and delivered by Hunter TAFE (the partner RTO). In 2017, the NSW Department of Premier and Cabinet joined Training Services NSW (Department of Industry) as one of the funders.

Participants are recommended by their schools and can be either students who have completed Year 10 and are willing to sign out of school to participate or Year 12 school leavers looking to gain technical STEM skills.

Figure 5.1. Designing STEMship

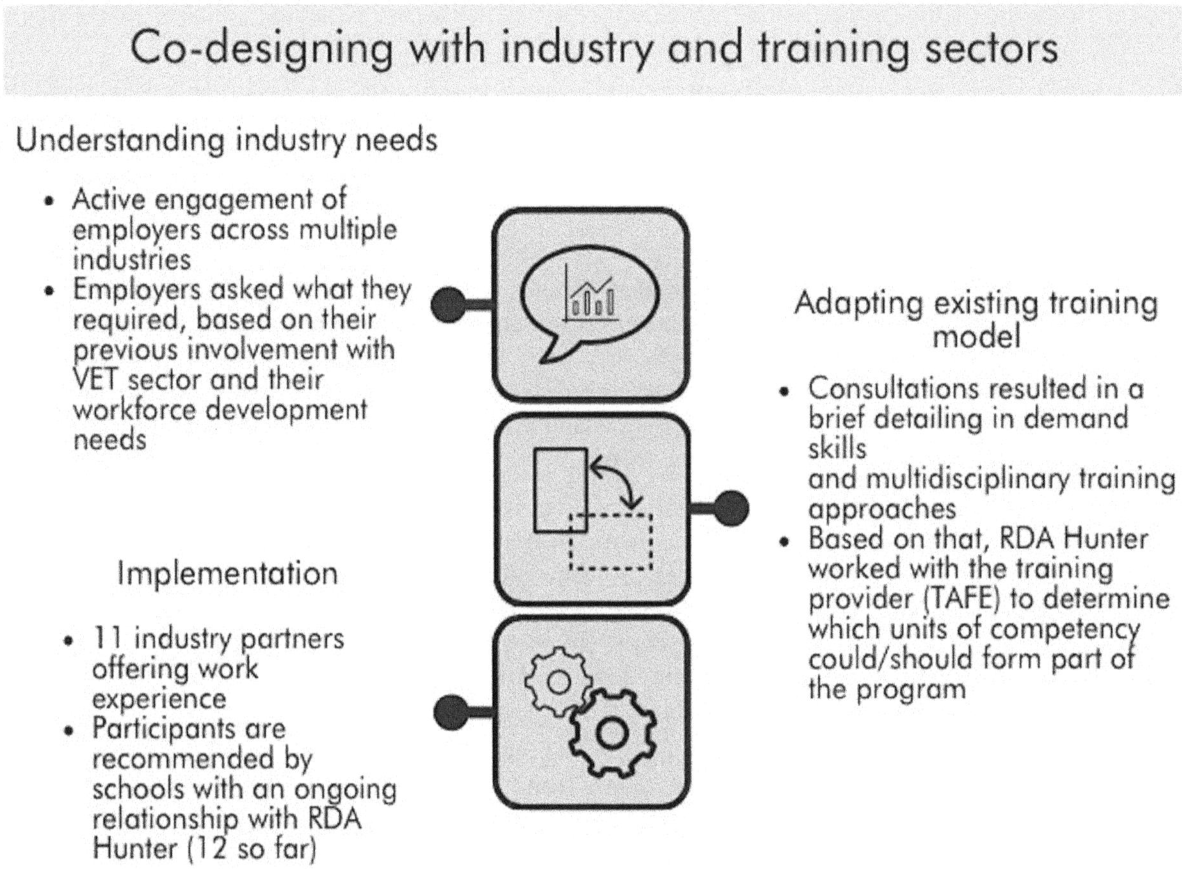

Source: Supplied by Author. Authors elaboration based on interviews with STEMship

Participants are exposed to a combination of work placements and post-secondary courses (units of competency) focusing on developing STEM capabilities, digital literacy, soft skills, and understanding of current industry workforce requirements. In-class training follows a multidisciplinary design, which allows students to gain skills from multiple training packages (19 units of competency across 7 different training packages). Learning is project-based, meaning students develop skills from different units of competency through a single project.

At the beginning of the programme, students visit all the industry partners to get a sense of what they do and their workplace expectations regarding ways of working. This interaction helps students identify which industry partners they would like to work with during the work placement component. Each student will work in one or more industry partners over a total of four weeks. Placements are flexible and depend on students' interests but also accommodate partners' needs in terms of numbers of students. Throughout the programme, participants receive integrated mentoring and pastoral care from the STEMship Coordinator (RDA Hunter) and key personnel within TAFE in a mix of individual and group settings to ensure they are progressing as expected and to understand and address specific needs to help them complete the programme.

Figure 5.2. STEMship elements

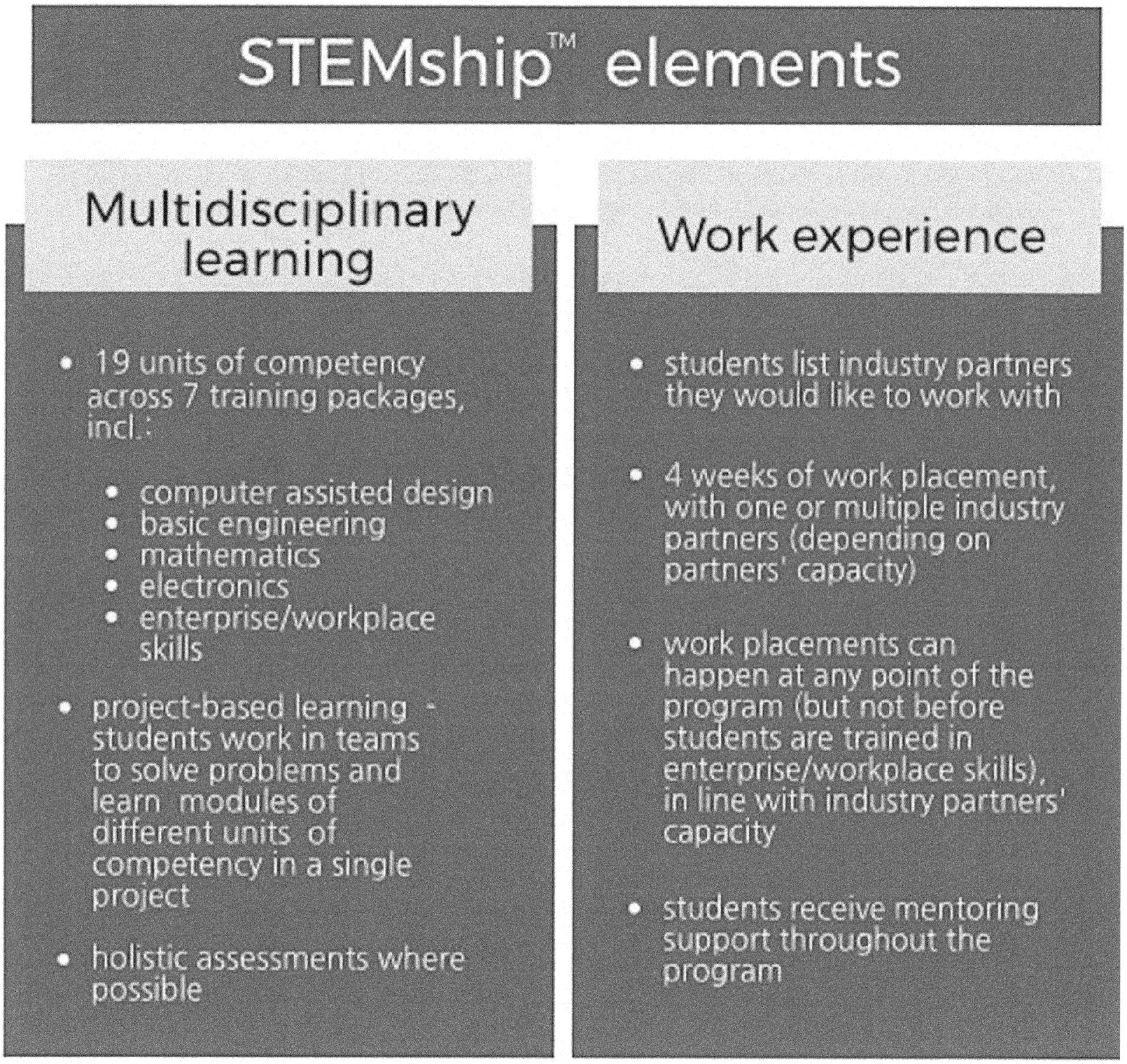

Source: Supplied by Author. Authors elaboration based on interviews with STEMship.

Programme Outcomes

The programme is in its second year, and it is still small in scale. Despite its relative youth and size, it has already generated positive outcomes for participants, most of which have engaged in apprenticeships after the programme, and industry participation has been increasing, with STEMship™ now seen as a key workforce development programme in the Hunter region. The programme constitutes an opportunity for students to complete a multi-disciplinary VET pre-vocational pathway; get exposure to a variety of industries via site visits and targeted work placements; develop highly attractive/employable digital and soft skills; gain awareness of current and future employment opportunities; get a taste of a variety of new and emerging industries and technologies. The programme also includes a full qualification in Certificate III Engineering-Technical.

For industry, the programmes allows them to develop a workforce that meets their requirements/needs; have access to a talent pool of work ready employees with STEM skills and capabilities; and promote their industry and career paths to prospective employees/apprentices.

For government, the programme enables them to promote VET pathways and emerging industries to schools, students and parents; attract talent to VET opportunities available under their 'Smart and Skilled' funding, especially in the 'Jobs of Tomorrow' (scholarship) qualifications; and create jobs and further enterprise opportunities in the Hunter region in high paying industries.

Table 5.1. Outcomes measured at 2 months following programme conclusion

	2016		2017	
	Number of students	%	Number of students	%
Commenced	18	-	16	-
Completed	16	89	15	94
	Of those who completed		**Of those who completed**	
Continued to an apprenticeship	8	50	10	67
Continued to other VET	3	19	5	33

Source: *Based on interviews regarding data provided to the author by STEMship*

Lessons learned

The pilot programme in 2016 and its subsequent iteration in 2017 saw the development and refinement of an innovative STEM based programme. There have been several key learnings from the first two iterations. Clear communication channels between STEMship™ students, parents, schools, RTO and industry partners are essential; A strategic approach is now taken to align course delivery dates with industry recruitment periods; The RTO component delivers better outcomes when it includes holistic assessment as well as integrated STEM skills application (i.e. multiple skills taught and assessed concurrently through project-based learning); and the timing of programme completion should ideally align with industry recruitment schedules. However, this is often challenging when engaging with a variety of business types and sizes, from start-ups, to SMEs to multinationals.

Drivers of success

Local leadership through RDA Hunter

RDA Hunter's economic development agenda focuses on advancing the region's innovation network and increasing the region's international competitiveness. To be able to achieve this, its *Smart Specialisation Strategy* articulates the importance of increasing the pool of the Hunter region's workforce with STEM, entrepreneurship and digital literacy skills (RDA Hunter, 2016[64]). Since 2009, through active engagement with business, universities, Hunter TAFE, schools, government agencies and community leaders, RDA

Hunter has a long track record of developing and delivering successful STEM education and workforce development programmes for students from primary to tertiary education. The maturity of these programmes has allowed RDA Hunter to gain trust and respect within the secondary school system in the region and encourage students to follow STEM based career pathways. It has also enabled RDA Hunter to effectively articulate industry needs to government and the training sector.

Partnership with industry

With the region's economy moving towards knowledge-intensive sectors and industries that traditionally do not engage with the VET sector, as well as a growing number of start-ups and SMEs, having industry actively involved in the design of the programme, has been key to attracting a diverse range of industry partners. Since students completing the programme are trained to industry standards and have had personal and professional engagement with industry partners, industry involvement also ensures enhanced transition for students into the workforce, therefore leveraging further outcomes for programme participants. The programme also aligns with industry policy at both state and federal levels, which facilitates engagement and partnerships with industry and government.

Implementation challenges

Current VET funding and delivery models

The programme is gaining traction in the Hunter region but scalability will depend on government funding (the programme is currently run on a contractual basis). A key challenge is aligning the traditional VET funding and delivery models to a multidisciplinary training model. Currently, government VET funding aligns to specific qualifications, which are occupation-based. Funding for multidisciplinary training already happens at university level, where students can graduate with a substantive proportion of elective units. Something similar would have to be adopted in the VET sector for the project to expand.

The way RTOs structure training delivery to align with the occupation-based model (i.e. single training package) also means that adopting the new model might be financially and administratively challenging. Delivering multiple training packages at once means drawing on more resources (i.e. trainers, equipment) per student than what is required by traditional VET courses in Australia. During the two years of STEMship™ delivery, TAFE NSW has been able to restructure resources, schedules and systems in an effective way, but other RTOs that might join the programme would also need to go through this challenging process of resource allocation.

References

Allen, R., N. Brasil and C. Manley (2017), *Future skills and training: A practical resource to help identify future skills and training*, https://www.aisc.net.au/sites/aisc/files/documents/Future Priority Skills Resource.pdf (accessed on 29 May 2018). [62]

Australian Bureau of Statistics (2018), *Detailed, Quarterly, cat. no. 6291.0.55.003, four quarter average of original data.* [57]

Australian Bureau of Statistics (2016), *1381.0.55.001 - Research Paper: A Review of Selected Regional Industrial Diversity Indexes, 2011*, http://www.abs.gov.au/ausstats/abs@.nsf/mf/1381.0.55.001 (accessed on 30 May 2018). [55]

Australian Bureau of Statistics (2015), *4250.0.55.005 - Perspectives on Education and Training: Australians with qualifications in science, technology, engineering and mathematics (STEM), 2010–11*, http://www.abs.gov.au/AUSSTATS/abs@.nsf/Lookup/4250.0.55.005Main+Features12010%E2%80%9311?OpenDocument (accessed on 29 May 2018). [59]

Australian Government Department of Jobs and Small Business (2018), *Skill Shortage List New South Wales*, https://docs.jobs.gov.au/system/files/doc/other/skillshortagelistnsw_9.pdf (accessed on 5 June 2018). [56]

Foundation for Young Australians (2017), *THE NEW WORK MINDSET: 7 New Job Clusters To Help Young People.* [63]

Prinsley, R. and K. Baranyai (2015), *Occasional Paper Series Issue 9 - STEM education and the workplace*, https://www.chiefscientist.gov.au/wp-content/uploads/OPS09_02Mar2015_Web.pdf (accessed on 29 May 2018). [60]

RDA Hunter (2016), *Smart Specialisation Strategy [S3] for the Hunter Region: A strategy for innovation-driven growth.* [64]

Snell, D., V. Gerkara and K. Gatt (2016), *Cross-Occupational Skill transferability: challenges and opportunities in a changing economy*, https://www.ncver.edu.au/__data/assets/file/0023/55913/cross-occupationalskilltransferability-2862.pdf (accessed on 30 May 2018). [61]

Startup Muster (2015), *Startup Muster 2015 Report.* [58]

STEMship (2017), *STEMSHIP IS AUSTRALIA'S FIRST VET PRE-EMPLOYMENT PROGRAM FOCUSING ON THE DEVELOPMENT OF STEM SKILLS AT A TECHNICAL LEVEL*, http://rdahunter.org.au/initiatives/stemship (accessed on 29 May 2018). [54]

Chapter 6. Targeting disadvantaged youth – Cowboys: Dream, Believe, Achieve Case Study

This case study provides an overview of a programme in Queensland, Australia, where a sports club has built on its local business and community networks to generate partnerships with training providers and employers to deliver individually tailored Vocational Education and Training (VET) in the hospital sector for disadvantaged and disengaged youth. In particular, the programme focused on Aboriginal and Torres Strait Islander to place them in higher quality jobs.

Background

The Dream, Believe, Achieve (DBA) programme, conceived by the North Queensland Cowboys rugby league club, operates in a region with relatively high levels of youth unemployment, especially amongst the Indigenous population. The programme focuses on creating tailored VET pathways within the hospitality sector to provide disadvantaged, at-risk, and long term unemployed job seekers with the opportunity to understand the value of and gain access to education and training, thereby enabling participants to achieve their employment goals.

Unemployment and skills gaps affect disadvantaged job seekers

Townsville is the largest city in Queensland, Australia with a population of 190 000 people. It is an export hub for the resources and agriculture industries, given its proximity to Asia. The economy has transitioned over recent years to a service-based economy, with employment growing fastest in service occupations. In December 2016, the Australian Government, the Queensland Government and the Townsville City Council signed Australia's first City Deal – a 15-year commitment, developed in collaboration with the Townsville community and private sector, to deliver economic and social outcomes for the region. Part of the Deal's commitments are the delivery of the North Queensland Stadium and the Townsville Entertainment and Convention Centre, both of which are expected to boost job creation and skills development in the construction, services, tourism, retail, commercial and hospitality industries (Australian Government Department of Infrastructure, Regional Development and Cities, 2018[65]).

Despite its economic potential, the region has seen slower job growth compared to the rest of Queensland and Australia (8% between 2011-2016, compared to 15% and 11% respectively) (REMPLAN, 2018[66]). Unemployment rates are slightly higher than the Queensland and national rates (9.3% in 2017, compared to 5.9% in Queensland and 5.4 % nationally, with the difference largely explained by high unemployment rates within the Aboriginal and Torres Strait Islander population (24% unemployment rate, compared to 7% for the non-Indigenous population in Townsville in 2016 (RDA Townsville and North West Australia, 2017[67]).

The Townsville region also experiences high levels of youth disengagement within the Aboriginal and Torres Strait Islander population. For example, only 30.3% of Aboriginal and Torres Strait Islander youth aged 18 to 24 years are engaged in work, study or training, compared to 68.9% of non-Indigenous Australian youth. Aboriginal and Torres Strait Islander youth disengagement is also higher than at state level, where it is at 63.9% (Queensland Government Statistician's Office, 2018[68]).

The root of these issues experienced by the Aboriginal and Torres Strait Islander traces back to family and cultural histories of unemployment and incarceration. A much higher percentage of Aboriginal and Torres Strait Islander youth and children live in jobless families (44.6%) compared to non-Indigenous Australian families (11.1%) (Queensland Government Statistician's Office, 2018[68]). On average, in 2015, Aboriginal and Torres Strait Islander adults are 13 times more likely to be incarcerated than non-Indigenous Australians. Aboriginal and Torres Strait Islander youth are sentenced to juvenile detention at approximately 24 times the rate of non-Indigenous Australian youth (Steering Committee for the Review of Government Service Provision, 2016[69]). These challenges combined with limited skills, education and employment experience make it difficult for

Aboriginal and Torres Strait Islander peoples to secure and maintain employment (Australian Institute of Health and Welfare, 2017[70]).

Figure 6.1. Causes of education and training challenges affecting Aboriginal and Torres Strait Islander adults and youth in Townsville

Source: Chappell, C. (2017), *Queensland Training Awards 2017 (2016/17): North Queensland Cowboys*; Queensland Government Statistician's Office (2018), *Queensland Regional Profiles: Indigenous Profile, RDA TNWQ region*, http://www.qgso.qld.gov.au (accessed on 18 January 2018).

The North Queensland Cowboys saw its local connections with business partners (mostly employers in the hospitality sector) as an opportunity to leverage Aboriginal and Torres Strait Islander employment. Through consultations with employers, registered training organisations (RTOs) and community service providers, the Club identified key challenges that Aboriginal and Torres Strait Islander faced in accessing VET courses and employment, including low language, literacy and numeracy skills, designed a training programme focused on addressing these challenges (Allara Learning, 2016[71]).

Education and training challenges within the current VET system

Townsville's accommodation and food services industry employs around 7% of the workforce (REMPLAN, 2018[72]). It has the highest rate of staff turnover, which creates employment opportunities for job seekers (Australian Government, 2017[73]). In 2016, a shortage of skilled hospitality workers with industry experience occurred both across the state of Queensland and nationally (Chamber of Commerce & Industry Queensland, 2016[74]; Colmar Brunton, 2016[75]).

National training quality standards require that students enrolled in a Certificate III in Hospitality complete 36 service periods (shifts) of practical work placement. Each service is a minimum of 2 hours in duration. This work experience is mostly undertaken in a campus-based café and/or restaurant (TAFE Queensland, 2018[76]). One of the challenges with this model is that students do not gain enough practical experience in the hospitality industry, having less chances of gaining a practical understanding of venue operating procedures, the different work hours, and the fluctuating nature of hospitality jobs in relation to the tourism sector (Colmar Brunton, 2016[75]). This creates a misalignment between training and employers' expectations in relation to customer service and job-readiness skills.

In a survey of tourism and hospitality careers undertaken on behalf of the Australian Trade Commission (Austrade), employers expressed that courses did not meet workplace needs; trainers lacked industry experience; coursework was too theoretical and did not provide enough focus on the development of practical skills; computer and IT skills were not provided to sufficient levels. (Colmar Brunton, 2016[75]).

Programme approach

The North Queensland Cowboys has operated in Townsville for 22 years. A community-based organisation, the Club uses its business and community networks to improve the lives of disadvantaged youth and at-risk job seekers in the region. In operation since 2012, the DBA programme draws both on these networks and on the unique brand power of the Cowboys to attract and engage programme participants and to provide training that is tailored to participants' and employers' needs.

The programme design is based on in-depth consultation with local industries and community sectors. The Club also operates a registered, community owned charity, Cowboys Community Foundation (CCF) that aims to "improve employment, health and social outcomes for young North Queenslanders through education-based programmes" (Cowboys Community Foundation, 2018[77]). Drawing on both the Club's and CCF's community and business connections, the DBA initiative was able to co-ordinate in-depth consultations with employers, employment services, community service providers, Indigenous organisations and leaders throughout the region, and registered training organisations. After this extensive consultation and analysis, the DBA programme was developed to focus on work experience placements with the Club's business partners, training tailored to student's individual needs, and intensive mentoring (Chappell, 2017[78]).

Funding for the DBA training programme is provided by the Queensland Government through its Skilling Queenslanders for Work initiative. The Initiative offers funding to not-for-profit community organisations that focus on providing VET opportunities to disadvantaged job seekers, disengaged youth, and at risk youth engaged with Youth Justice Services or Queensland Corrective Services (Queensland Government Department of Employment, Small Business and Training, 2018[79]). The DBA programme currently focuses on delivering the nationally recognised Certificate III in Hospitality. Training has been tailored to local employers' needs, with the goal of ensuring that all participants are job ready, adequately equipped with industry experience, and have highly-developed customer service skills. Workplace-based experience in one of the Club's partners is provided as a central part of the course. Students work as trainees with individual employers, including at Cowboys events such as game days and corporate hospitality events at the 1300 SMILES Stadium.

Intensive mentoring

Participants receive up to 12 months' individual mentoring and support. Once a DBA programme participant has been identified, an Aboriginal or Pacific Islander mentor is assigned as a case manager. All mentors working on the DBA are recruited by the Cowboys to specifically work with programme participants. Mentors work with participants to understand their career aspirations and identify any barriers to training participation and future employment. Common barriers are difficulties in accessing stable housing and/or transport, health issues, and foundation skills or learning gaps.

Mentors provide support throughout the duration of the course by assisting participants to find industry-based work experience and preparing them for job applications and interviews. At the end of the course, mentors link participants with potential employment opportunities. Support continues once students gain employment to ensure that the student and employer are able to work through any initial problems that may occur. This support by the programme mentors and the employers provides a stable introduction to the work environment and the development of sustainable employment for students.

Individually tailored training

The Cowboys and partner RTO, Allara Learning, work together to deliver a training model that is "responsive to each participant's learning style and pace" (Chappell, 2017[78]). This means that the Certificate III in Hospitality course units of competency are selected to best suit the needs of the participating cohort, based on the mentors' assessments. The course delivery is composed of intensive in-class training, complemented by out-of-class tutoring and support provided by Cowboys' mentors.

Course study units are selected based on the identified needs of the training cohort. For example, English is a second language for Aboriginal and Torres Strait Islander peoples and some students have learning challenges and personal barriers that impact on their ability to attend classes, complete the course and transition into employment. In this circumstance, mentors provide language, literacy and numeracy (LLN) tutoring support for participants for the duration of the course. For assessments, the RTO applies 'reasonable adjustment' for these students so that they have equal opportunities to prove competency in learning. For example, for participants who have difficulty in expressing knowledge in writing, oral assessment can be offered as an alternative (Queensland Government Department of Employment, Small Business and Training, 2018[80]).

Others, in particular those who were long term unemployed, lack understanding of employer's expectations, and how to apply and prepare for jobs. The introduction of job-readiness focused training, such as timeliness and practices for when running late and calling in sick, and resume and cover letter writing and interview preparation is incorporated into the training package. Mentors then tutor students during out-of-class hours to assist them with their skills development.

Additionally, all in-class training is conducted by professional trainers who are experienced at teaching disadvantaged job seekers and have well developed cultural awareness, sensitivity and respect for Aboriginal and Torres Strait Islander people's culture. These are examples of how a VET course can be tailored to suit the needs of individual students whilst still conforming to the delivery of required units of competency. It is these considerations of flexible delivery methods that enable the DBA to offer training that matches the capacities and needs of each person.

As another way of motivating and engaging participants, the Club offers Cowboys merchandise, game day tickets, membership, and opportunities to meet Cowboys players (present and past) to DBA trainees as rewards. Participants' progress and milestone goals are celebrated through group activities, which contributes toward an increase in self-esteem and ongoing motivation to complete the course and gain employment.

Figure 6.2. DBA solutions to provide disadvantaged job seekers with access to education and training opportunities

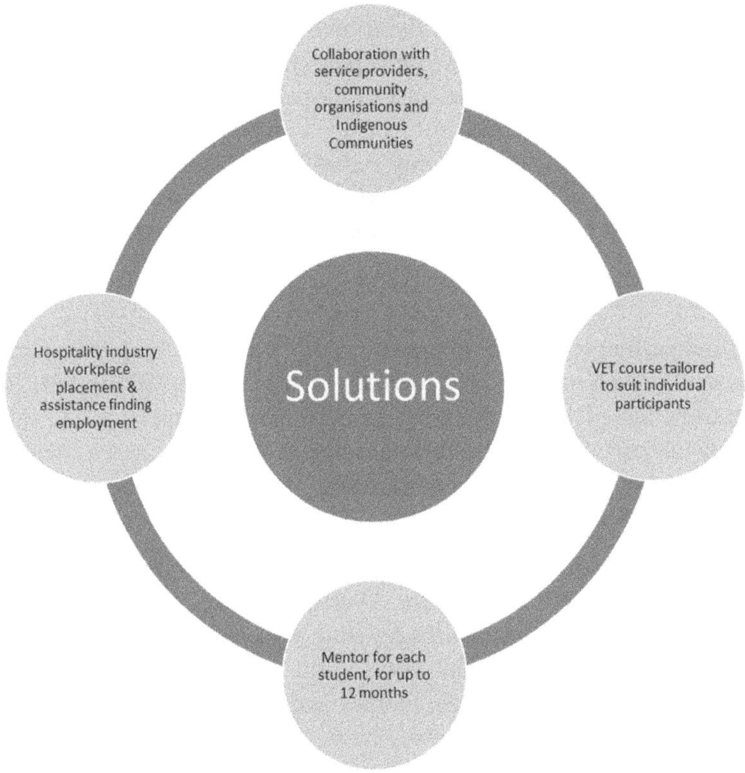

Note: An overview of the solutions developed by the Dream, Believe, Achieve initiative to provide access to education and training for disadvantaged jobs seekers in the Townsville region.
Source: Allara Learning (2016), *North Queensland Cowboys team up with Allara Learning to build careers & future*, http://allaralearning.com.au/casestudies/item/north-queensland-cowboys-team-up-with-allara-learning (accessed on 19 January 2018); Chappell, C. (2017), *Queensland Training Awards 2017 (2016/17): North Queensland Cowboys*.

Programme outcomes

The Dream Believe Achieve programme is in its fifth year of operation. The Cowboys, in partnership with registered RTO, Allara Learning, have been delivering a Certificate III in Hospitality for three years. Although small in scale, the hospitality programme has generated positive outcomes for participants in Townsville. This has resulted in the expansion of the DBA programme to the city of Cairns, Queensland.

Over the two years that the DBA programme has operated, 100% of the programme's training commencement target was achieved, and 81.8% of students completed the Certificate III in Hospitality, against the programme's benchmark of 80%. Of those students who completed the DBA programme, currently 45.9% of students have gained employment. These employment figures are in alignment with national averages. A 2016 report produced by the National Centre for Vocational Education Research (NCVER) investigated Indigenous VET participation, completion and outcomes over the past decade. It was reported that in 2015-16, nationally 45% of Indigenous graduates who were unemployed prior to commencing their course gained employment after course completion (Windley, 2017[81]). In the field of hospitality, food and personal services, nationally 55.4% of Indigenous VET graduates gained employment after course completion (Windley, 2017[81]). The DBA employment rate is marginally higher than the national average, which reflects the success of the programme, after only three years of operation.

The number of DBA students who continued with further VET quadrupled from 5% in 2016 to 20.2% in 2017. NCVER's analysis on national VET graduates not employed before engaging in training, showed that 34.3% of students went on to enrol in further study in 2016 (NCVER, 2017[82]). These results highlight the progress and positive impact of the DBA programme for participants. For full breakdown of DBA 2016-2017 training results see Table 6.1.

Table 6.1. Outcomes for the Dream, Believe, Achieve 2016-2017 training period

	2016		2017*	
	Number of students	%	Number of students	%
Commenced	61	-	104	-
Completed certificate III	48	78.6	87	83.6
Awarded certificate of attainment	61	100	104	100
	After training outcomes	%	**After training outcomes**	%
Gained employment	26	42.6%	36*	34.6%
Continued to other VET training	5	8.2%	21	20.2%
Unknown	30	49.2%	47	45.2%

Note: *2017 cohort to date. January 2018, some students are still completing training.

The DBA programme provides pathways to education and employment for disengaged youth and disadvantaged and long term unemployed job seekers that were not previously available to them. Students are able to gain transferable skills, such as job-readiness and excellence in customer service; mentoring support and employment aspiration planning for up to 12 months assistance with assessing and overcoming barriers to accessing VET opportunities; confidence in their skills and abilities, which is an important factor for students from a disadvantaged background; exposure to the hospitality industry and different real-world work environments; and develop highly desired entry-level practical and knowledge-based skills that ensure they are job ready.

The DBA programme also has positive outcomes for the hospitality sector in Townville and local regional areas, with the Club effectively aligning training providers' offerings to local employers' needs. Through the programme, employers gain a much-needed entry-level workforce that is both suitably trained and job ready; the opportunity to promote the hospitality industry and the various career pathways available to those prospective employees; and the opportunity to provide practical work placement/employment to a sector of the community that has largely reduce employment opportunities, thereby contributing to the community as a whole.

Lessons learned

The first two years of the DBA programme enabled the re-development of the programme's initial processes, from student commencement through to course completion. Key learning areas addressed were the VET curriculum and training delivery, student readiness for study, work experience placement, and student recruitment. The investment in and development of a collaborative approach with industry and community organisations resulted in a tailored solution to delivering the Certificate III in hospitality. The key challenges and drivers of success are discussed below.

Challenges

The provision of flexible and tailored training is a learning curve, with the approach to VET requiring constant modification and fine-tuning to accommodate individual participants and their learning needs. Student recruitment was particularly challenging in the early stages of the programme. Initially, participants registered for the DBA programme out of training obligations but had no real desire to search for employment or complete further study. The interview process was refined to better identify participants who genuinely sought employment and the opportunity to further their skills.

Drivers of success

Cowboys brand and community leadership

The North Queensland Cowboys provide a sense of identity, social cohesion and local pride in the Townsville area. The Cowboys embody the North Queensland culture and provide inspiration for young people throughout the region. Game days are a strong part of the local culture. All players in the under 20's squad must either be furthering their education or be employed. The Club's focus on youth education and training provides a positive outlook for young people in Townsville.

Having operated for 22 years, the Cowboys have developed many connections to local industry, community and youth through their sporting events and education and training programmes. The range of programmes offered encompasses primary school years and encouraging school attendance, motivating and supporting secondary school Aboriginal and Torres Strait Islander students to complete their education, and culminating in the Dream, Believe, Achieve programme that provides disadvantaged job seekers with VET and employment opportunities. The development of these programmes has enabled the Cowboys to gain the trust and respect of schools, training providers and community organisations.

Collaboration with industry and community organisations

The breadth of the Cowboys' community and industry networks provides the Club with a unique position to understand and respond to changes and unmet needs in the community. Through the many programmes that it offers to youth, in a sporting capacity and education and training capacity, the Club is actively involved in the community. This gives the Club first hand insights into community needs and to build relationships.

The Club leverages its relationships with corporate sponsors to promote the DBA initiative, which has resulted in active engagement from the business sector in Townsville. The Club has established five programmes that focus on education and training, and the transition to employment for young people and the disadvantaged. The Cowboys Community

Foundation provides additional access to community networks in the region. The NRL Cowboys House programme focuses on Aboriginal and Torres Strait Islander students, a group most at risk of not achieving their potential. This programme promotes collaboration and engagement with Aboriginal and Torres Strait Islander communities and Elders in and around the Townsville region.

Involvement by the Club with the Townsville community, and Aboriginal and Torres Strait Islander communities and Traditional Owners in the region, has resulted in valuable input about unmet community needs. Networking with employers identified employment needs, and industry and trade trends. The extensive collaboration with community and employers enabled the DBA initiative to plan and implement training programmes that provide employment for disadvantaged job seekers in the region.

References

Allara Learning (2016), *North Queensland Cowboys team up with Allara Learning to build careers & future*, http://allaralearning.com.au/casestudies/item/north-queensland-cowboys-team-up-with-allara-learning (accessed on 19 January 2018). [71]

Australian Government (2017), *Understanding the Townsville jobs market*, https://docs.jobs.gov.au/system/files/doc/other/townsville_jobactive_fact_sheet_final_access.pdf. [73]

Australian Government Department of Infrastructure, Regional Development and Cities (2018), *Smart Cities Plan: The Townsville City Deal*, https://citydeals.infrastructure.gov.au/townsville (accessed on 17 January 2018). [65]

Australian Institute of Health and Welfare (2017), *7.5 Income and employment for Indigenous Australians*, https://www.aihw.gov.au/getmedia/2f327206-c315-43a7-b666-4fe24fefc12f/aihw-australias-welfare-2017-chapter7-5.pdf.aspx (accessed on 19 January 2018). [70]

Chamber of Commerce & Industry Queensland (2016), *Hospitality industry: skills and labour shortages*, CCIQ News, https://www.cciq.com.au/news/hospitality-industry-skills-and-labour-shortages (accessed on 18 January 2018). [74]

Chappell, C. (2017), *Queensland Training Awards 2017 (2016/17): North Queensland Cowboys*. [78]

Colmar Brunton (2016), *Tourism and Hospitality Careers Report*, https://www.austrade.gov.au/ArticleDocuments/5499/Tourism-and-Hospitality-Careers-Report-2016.pdf.aspx. [75]

Cowboys Community Foundation (2018), *Cowboys Community Foundation*. [77]

NCVER (2017), *VET graduate outcomes 2017: infographic*, National Centre for Vocational Education Research (NCVER), https://ncver.edu.au/data/data/infographics/vet-graduate-outcomes-2017-infographic (accessed on 19 January 2018). [82]

Queensland Government Department of Employment, Small Business and Training (2018), *Reasonable Adjustment in teaching, learning and assessment for learners with a disability*, https://training.qld.gov.au/site/providers/Documents/inclusive/disability/reasonable-adjustment-for-web.pdf. [80]

Queensland Government Department of Employment, Small Business and Training (2018), *Skilling Queenslanders for Work for training providers*, Queensland Government Training, https://training.qld.gov.au/providers/funded/sqw (accessed on 18 January 2018). [79]

Queensland Government Statistician's Office (2018), *Queensland Regional Profiles: Indigenous Profile, RDA TNWQ region*, http://www.qgso.qld.gov.au (accessed on 18 January 2018). [68]

RDA Townsville and North West Australia (2017), *Local government are unemployment rate, Townsville*, http://rdanwq.org.au/regional-profile. [67]

REMPLAN (2018), *Townsville North Queensland: Employment by Industry*, http://www.economyprofile.com.au/townsvillenorthqueensland/industries/employment (accessed on 18 January 2018). [72]

REMPLAN (2018), *Townsville North Queensland: Unemployment Rate*, https://www.economyprofile.com.au/townsvillenorthqueensland/trends/unemployment#table (accessed on 15 January 2018). [66]

Steering Committee for the Review of Government Service Provision (2016), *Overcoming Indigenous Disadvantage: Key Indicators 2016 - Overview*, https://www.pc.gov.au/research/ongoing/overcoming-indigenous-disadvantage/2016/report-documents/oid-2016-overcoming-indigenous-disadvantage-key-indicators-2016-overview.pdf. [69]

TAFE Queensland (2018), *Certificate III in Hospitality (SIT30616)*, TAFE Queensland course guide, https://tafeqld.edu.au/courses/17724/certificate-iii-in-hospitality (accessed on 17 January 2018). [76]

Windley, G. (2017), *Indigenous VET participation, completion and outcomes: change over the past decade*, https://www.ncver.edu.au/__data/assets/pdf_file/0031/484447/Indigenous-VET-participation,-completion-and-outcomes.pdf. [81]

Chapter 7. Embedding skills training in economic development – Collective Education in Tasmania Case Study

This chapter provides information on a programme case study from Tasmania that targets Year 12 completion of education by bringing together local schools and employers to co-design and co-deliver skills development programmes that align with industry practice. The programme targets at-risk youth who typically do not finish Year 12 and are at-risk for being locked out of the labour market.

Background

Tasmania's recent economic and labour market performance

Tasmania has enjoyed positive economic success in recent years. Government and Industry sources indicate economic and employment growth to be stronger than previously experienced (Eslake, 2016[83]; Parliament of Tasmania, 2017[84]). The main industries, in terms of contribution to GSP (Gross State Product) growth in 2015-2016 were agriculture, health care and social assistance, construction, professional and technical services, and transport, postal and warehousing services. Household income growth has been driven by the income growth of Tasmania's small to medium enterprise (SME) sector (Eslake, 2016[83]; Parliament of Tasmania, 2017[84]). Tasmania has a lower GSP compared to the rest of Australia - three factors can explain the gap:

- **Employment gap:** fewer Tasmanians have a job compared to the national average – this accounted for 41% of the difference in per capita gross product in 2014-2015 (Eslake, 2016[83]).
- **Working hours gap:** employed Tasmanians work fewer hours than the national average – this accounted for 41% of the difference in per capita gross product in 2014-2015. In August 2015, 12% of employed Tasmanians were working fewer hours than they wanted to (3 percentage points above the national average) (Eslake, 2016[83]).
- **Productivity gap:** the value of Tasmanians' production per hour worked is lower than the national average – this accounted for 18% of the difference in per capita gross product in 2014-2015. For a majority of Tasmanian industries (apart from agriculture; electricity, gas and water supply; transport; and retailing) labour productivity is below the corresponding national industry average (Eslake, 2016[83]).

Nevertheless, in 2014-2015, employment grew by an average of 3%, twice the national average, after having continuously decreased between 2011 and 2014. The unemployment rate has also declined, and was close to the national average in 2015 (around 6%). However, this is the product not only of employment growth, but also declining labour force participation. Youth unemployment was also higher than the national average (16% compared to 13% in the year to October 2015). Low historical averages of the Australian Dollar and improved business confidence indicate that growth is likely to be sustained in the near-term. Access to a suitably qualified workforce will be paramount for Tasmania to take full advantage of emerging economic growth prospects.

Challenges within the current education system

Student retention, education attainment and future work and education participation are all areas of critical interest for the Beacon Foundation's Collective Ed initiative. This initiative exists within the context of educational reform by the Tasmanian Government to improve students' retention and attainment. These reforms aim to frame the future of the Tasmanian education system. A selection of the reform areas is described below.

Student attainment

In 2013, 83% of the population aged 20-24 in Tasmania had attained at least Year 12 or equivalent or Australian Qualification Framework (AQF) Certificate II or above, compared to 87% for the whole of Australia; and 81% had attained at least Year 12 or AQF Certificate III or above, compared to 86% in Australia (ACARA, 2013[85]). Data from the *Report on Government Services 2015* (Productivity Commission) shows that students engaged in full-time education in Tasmania complete Year 12 less often than students in other states/territories (except the Northern Territory) regardless of remoteness or socio-economic status (SES) (Eslake, 2016[83]). Although it is true that students of lower SES generally have lower Year 12 completion rates (not only in Tasmania but throughout Australia), Tasmanian students of low SES perform worse than their counterparts in other parts of Australia, as do Tasmanian students from medium and high SES backgrounds compared to their respective counterparts (Eslake, 2016[83]).

On average, Australian students living in remote areas perform as well as those living in provincial areas, but both perform worse than those living in metropolitan areas. In Tasmania students' performance worsens with the level of remoteness, and students living in any of these areas perform worse than their counterparts in the rest of Australia, apart from those in the Northern Territory (Eslake, 2016[83]).

Student retention

ABS data shows Tasmania performed poorly in retention rates compared to the whole of Australia. According to the data, 72% of students in Tasmania progressed from Year 10 to Year 12, compared with 83% of all Australian students (Australian Bureau of Statistics, 2016[86]).

Participation in education and work

Tasmania has a higher proportion of youth at risk (people aged 15-24 not engaged in formal employment or training) compared to the whole of Australia. In 2015, 75% of Tasmanians aged 15-24 were fully engaged through formal study and/or employment, compared to 80% nationally (Australian Bureau of Statistics, 2016[87]). Looking at the 20-24 year old age bracket, in 2013 only 64% of 20-24 year olds in Tasmania were fully engaged through education and/or employment, compared to 74% in Australia.

Recent direction and areas of education reform in Tasmania

Education Bill 2016

The Education Bill 2016 brings together three previously separate pieces of legislation and includes some significant reforms of the Tasmanian education system (Parliament of Tasmania, 2016[88]). One of the central reforms proposed is changes to leaving requirements which will require students to complete Year 12, attain a Certificate III, or have turned 18 years old.

Extending government high schools

As part of the Tasmanian Government's plan to increase high school retention rates in the State, rural and regional high schools were encouraged to extend their delivery to Year 12. The first six of these schools commenced delivery of Years 11-12 in 2015, with an additional seven commencing in 2016. In the Tasmanian Government's Department of Education Annual Report for 2016/17 a total of 30 schools (55% of all high schools) were reported to be delivering Years 11 and 12 (Tasmanian Government Department of Education, 2017[89]). A further eight schools will commence extension to their services during 2018.

Years 11 and 12 curriculum website

This website contains curriculum support materials and aims to inform teachers and school leaders of developments and opportunities in the Years 11 and 12 cohort including learning opportunities, support for moderation and assessment and professional readings (Tasmanian Government Department of Education, 2018[90]).

My Education initiative

Central to *My Education* is an online portal providing students with access to a variety of resources, material and data they can access and use in developing a life and career plan (Tasmanian Government Department of Education, 2018[91]). *My Education* is an approach to career education that guides Tasmanian students from Kindergarten to Year 12. It supports students to identify their personal interests, values, strengths and aspirations, and teaches them how to use this knowledge to make decisions about their future learning, work and life opportunities. It is a whole school approach, grounded in partnership between the student, parents and carers, the school and the community, and also aims to engage with business and industry in Tasmania by linking education with a student's future employment options.

Programme approach

Braving a 'systems change' approach

Collective Ed is about building a new system of practise and being able to demonstrate and share its learnings, outcomes and achievements. The project is a *living lab* of community actors coming together with a commitment to try something innovation. Developed in community partnership, Collective Ed is a Beacon Foundation state-wide initiative built from best and emerging practise in human-centred, collaborative design and adaptive leadership. Its funding comes from Australia's largest philanthropic fund, the Paul Ramsay Foundation, and the Tasmanian State Government via its Departments of Education, and State Growth.

Collective Ed is a systematic approach to achieving collective understanding and commitment to common goals, by re-emphasising working alongside schools as they begin to undertake an outward-facing approach to their planning.

The Collective Ed vision

The vision for Collective Ed is a future where: "Tasmanian communities are innovative, connected and thriving; and The Tasmanian education system continues to adapt to meet the opportunities of the 21st century"; where: students are healthy, have a voice and are engaged in learning; teachers are innovative and connected; parents value and support education; community is networked and collaborative; and business and industry are active participants in education. The Foundation's leadership is clear that its goals are not to deliver and manage change but rather to enhance the capacity of community actors to define and achieve their own success.

Changing the game from deep foundations

The Collective Ed model is the product of the Foundation's many years of operating in Tasmania. For almost 30 years, Beacon has taken a co-construction approach to the development of what it describes as *real-world education* through partnerships between schools and industry. Using the Beacon model, they enable Australian students' access to industry-relevant curriculum; work experience placements; work readiness training; and direct pathways into employment. The model advocates a place-based, human-centred, collaborative working and collective impact approach (Collaboration for Impact, 2017[92]).

At the Foundation level, Beacon creates employment and education opportunities for young people via their schools and business communities through activities such as: Business Blackboards, Collaborative Classrooms, Site Tours, Speed Careering, Work Experience; and Mock Interviews This encompassed school-based preparation and hands-on experience with an employer which led to specific employment opportunities. Programmes that have emerged from the Beacon model also include:

- Real Futures Generation: This encompassed school-based preparation and hands-on experience with an employer which led to specific employment opportunities (Beacon Foundation, 2018[93]).
- MyRoad via eBeacon: a digital online platform which extends the reach of its resources and the mentorship capacity of its industry partners and volunteers (Beacon Foundation, 2018[94]).

Table 7.1. An overview of Beacon model components

High Impact Programs	Beacon offers a series of one-day Work Readiness Programmes, targeted to specific age groups spanning Years 7 -12. Each program is designed to prepare students for a successful transition from school, through the development of 21st century skills that employers are looking for. Industry representatives share their stories and career journeys and encourage students to recognise their own potential.
Business Partnership Groups	Key stakeholders from schools, businesses and community groups come together and create a community-owned shared vision for change, and implement their plans throughout the year through a series of activities.
Industry Site Tours	Employers have a massive impact on the lives of young people by offering inspiring work exposure programmes. Employer-driven workplace experiences are undertaken by students and teachers, leading to increased industry knowledge and 21st Century job skills of participants for potential jobs.
Business Blackboards	Co-designed experiential learning for students, created by business people and classroom teachers working together. Business people bring the curriculum to life when presenting the lesson, applying authentic industry practices, sharing their own experiences and promoting specific job opportunities and career paths within their industry.
Speed Careers	This fast-paced, interactive session provides students or teachers with relevant and up-to-date, first-hand information about future career options from business representatives in the local community in a 'speed dating' format. Includes Careers on Wheels and Teacher Speed Careering.
Student Ambassador Programme	Beacon Student Ambassadors, elected from within the student body, take a leadership role in implementing the Beacon approach in the school and community.
Charter Signing Events	Students participate in a signature community event, publicly signing a board to signify their pledge that by the following year, they will continue in education, employment or training.
Work Exploration and Careers Education	Activities and events which prepare the students for the world of work; includes Mock Interviews, Work Experience and Work Shadowing and can be uniquely tailored events to suit a school's needs.

Note: Each component is selected and/or adapted to meet the needs of the specific school community.
Source: Detailed in interviews with Beacon staff and materials provided to the author by Beacon Real Futures Generation (Tasmania, 2011-2015)

Real Futures Generation (RFG) – Tasmania, 2011-2015

During 2011-15, 94 students were reported to have been employed as a result of their participation in the RFG programme, with 26 businesses operating in Tasmania being involved in the development/ hiring of the students. It is important to recognise that the young people participating in a Beacon programme are typically described as at-risk of disengagement from education and/or employment, with the vast majority living in communities experiencing socio-economic disadvantage.

Figure 7.1. National-level breakdown (including Tasmania) of position types resulting from the RFG programme

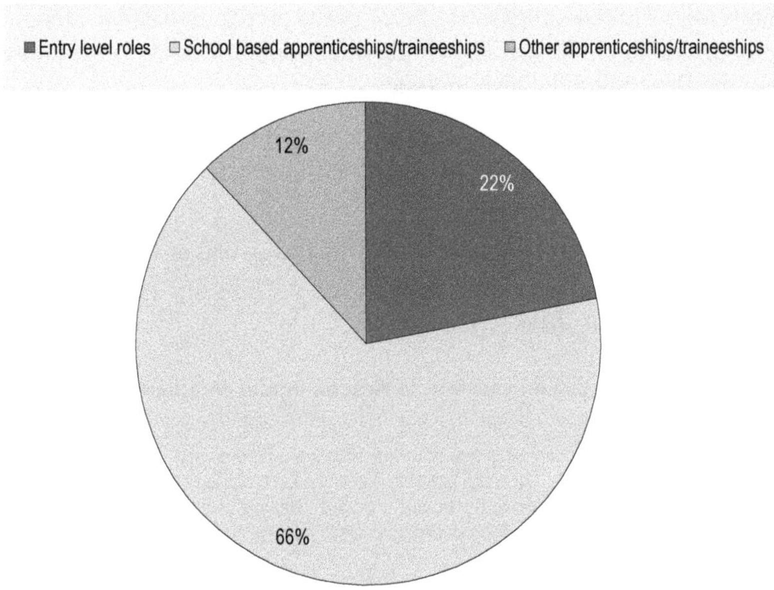

Note: This data was prepared as part of Beacon's report to the Australian Government Department of Education and Training in December 2014. The programme continued in Tasmania until later in 2015, when it was replaced by the Tasmanian Government funded Industry Pathway Program (IPP) project.
Source: Beacon Foundation (2014), Beacon Foundation Real Futures Generation Project. RFG value in focus: Collaborating with Tasmanian childcare sectors to connect young Tasmanians with meaningful futures.

RFG value in focus: Collaborating with Tasmanian childcare sectors to connect young Tasmanians with meaningful futures

In Tasmania, supply-side challenges surrounding Early Childhood Education and Care (ECEC) skills and workforce shortages inspired the engagement of Beacon's Real Futures Generation (RFG) approach. The pilot, involving the collaboration of Tasmanian Department of Education, Early Childhood Australia, and several ECEC centres, took a co-ordinated industry approach based on its Work Preparation Funnel approach. The pilot targeted Year 10-12 students, promoted ECEC career opportunities, and provided several school-based traineeships which involved undertaking a Certificate III in ECEC, employment at an ECEC centre and completion of a secondary school education. The traineeships were aligned to the Australian School-based Apprenticeships (ASBAs) system.

Table 7.2. ECEC pilot components

ECEC Career Awareness Program (CAP)	2-day workshop marketed to all Government High Schools (65 schools) – 20 schools were invited to participate. CAP emphasised ECEC career information and employment opportunities including ASBAs, a literacy and numeracy assessment, and offered 1-day work experience at an ECEC centre.
Parent/student information ECEC career sessions	Critical to this whole of community approach, students and their parents are invited to participate so that an encouraging and informed environment can be created. This contributes to student capacity to engage more meaningfully in ECEC employment and/or traineeships.
Industry Site Tours	Built upon its High Impact Program (HIP) knowledge, work readiness skills are taught to enable active participation by students in future ECEC work experience placements/ traineeships and job application processes.
Business Blackboards	Students who register for the Prepare for Work session are invited to apply for a one-week ECEC work placement. This is undertaken at a participating ECEC centre and is completed during the school term.
ECEC ASBA applications	The co-developed RFG approach leads to a rise in quality and volume of ASBAs received by the ECEC sector.

Note: ECEC pilot details as described to the author in conversation with Beacon. One of the participating ECEC organisations also detail the initiative

Source: Beacon Foundation (2014), Beacon Foundation Real Futures Generation Project; Goodstart Early Learning (2017), *Creating pathways to success through school-based apprenticeships*, https://www.goodstart.org.au/news-and-advice/April-2017/Creating-pathways-to-success-through-school-based (accessed on 23 May 2018).

High Impact Programs (Tasmania, 2017)

During 2017, 953 students and 77 educators from Tasmanian secondary schools worked with participants from 254 businesses. Educators and businesses reported support for the value of the programme and its alignment with education and labour market needs, and relevance for students as they look to enter the world of work. Similarly, when students were asked "How valuable was today's programme for you?" 21% (195 students) elected to describe it as life-changing, and 77% (716) said it was valuable.

HIP value in focus: Public sector job creation for young Tasmanians

In 2016, 80 students across three Tasmanian secondary schools engaged in work readiness development sessions with the support of a Foundation partner, MyState. In a related development, the Head of the State Service in Tasmania approved 20 school-based apprenticeships or traineeships across its own departments and agencies. This commitment will be realised in partnership with Beacon and the Tasmanian Department of Education and provide employment and learning pathways within the Tasmanian State Service agencies via the Australian school-based apprenticeship (ASBA) system.

MyRoad - Tasmania, August – December 2017

During 2017, MyRoad engaged 326 students from Tasmanian secondary schools, and 95 mentors from across 39 businesses based in Tasmania. After their MyRoad sessions, participating students are asked for their feedback. When asked *How valuable was today's programme for you?* 79% (234 students) said it was *valuable,* with a further 7% (23 students) describing it as *life-changing*.

MyRoad via eBeacon value in focus: Using technology to expanding programme reach.

MyRoad is designed for young women in their senior years of secondary school. The programme is built upon the understanding that mentoring is a contributing factor for young people and their future engagement in education and employment, in particular, where young people are at risk of disengagement (Bruce and Bridgeland, 2014[95]). Using video chat technology, Beacon facilitates and enables the engagement of industry mentors and their connection with young people. More than a mentor-matching service, structured learning models designed to develop key school transition skills are followed.

Lessons Learned

Lessons developed from Beacon's programme include: engagement with whole of family/community; pedagogical and educational expertise are critical; active creation of first-job opportunities is the role of the whole community; and planning for knowledge translation is central for programme sustainability and replication. With all of this in mind, The Beacon Foundation along with its Collective Ed partners is pursuing a model, which brings Tasmanian students and schools, their community and families, and businesses and employers more closely aligned in co-building their futures of work and education.

Beacon places great emphasis on the commitment and openness demonstrated by participating schools as they come on board with the initiative. This case study was developed shortly after its formal Collective Ed announcement in November 2017, which celebrated the participation of the following Tasmania public-sector schools: Port Dalrymple School; Deloraine High School; and Sorell High School. These schools joined the three pilot schools: Ulverstone High School, Jordan River Learning Federation and Bayview Secondary College.

Ways to enable systems change thinking and participation

Leverage credibility to secure financial sustainability

Longer-term commitment by funders, stakeholders, community, schools and/or businesses is always advantageous. This time allows space for approach consistency, and therefore truer tests of concept, design and implementation. To operate in this strategic manner is not easy, especially for not-for-profits and/or charity organisations where funding scarcity and operational commitments can divert critical resources and intelligence. Consolidation of existing knowledge, relationships and partnerships strengthens credibility and capacity to engage would-be funders and advocates. A clear sense of one's value, practise, and approach is paramount – know who you are and what you are about.

The right kind of funder matters – look beyond the monetary value

The Paul Ramsay Foundation, and the Tasmanian Government Departments of Education and Training and State Growth, fund the Collective Ed initiative. Both the value and duration of the funding commitment is remarkable with a total allocation of $15 million being made available to the Beacon Foundation from 2017-2021. All partnership actors commit to participation across the initiatives various phases, and there is a real acceptance that *all* partners are involved in the reshaping of this complex, interwoven system. There is a critical openness and willingness to reimagine a collective future built upon collective wisdom and aspiration.

Nothing can be achieved when goals are framed in a vacuum

Improved Year 12 attainment is a principal outcome goal, but this is built within a logic that educational, socio-economic and employment outcomes are inextricably linked. Importantly all actors express a willingness to co-create knowledge to enable real system mobility and benefit felt by community and industry. To enhance the discipline of the initiative's learning approach, Beacon has also engaged expertise from Tasmania's tertiary sector and specialists in developmental evaluation and collaboration to create an embedded monitoring, evaluation, learning and reporting approach. The initiative design represents great practise in re-imagining education and economic policy, and as Beacon's CEO, Scott Harris puts it "educating differently".

Change is political, it requires commitment to people.

You could say the climate was 'just right'. Beacon had the credibility, The Paul Ramsay Foundation had the funding commitment, and the Tasmanian government had a vision for a real change through strong leadership at the political and departmental level. Collective Ed seeks to act as a facilitator of systems change, rather than adopt the role of system leader or manager. Data generated, lessons learned and relationships developed will all be central to giving this transformed system the licence to operate.

Leverage the collective commitment – and resist the seduction of quick wins

For a sustainable system to prevail, the indicators of success must continue to communicate to the hearts and minds as well as the balance sheets of participating partners. The momentum built by the system-change mind-set is central to sustaining the energy and commitment of its participants, especially when the process of change can present challenges and obstacles. The obvious temptation to achieve some '*quick wins*' should be satisfied with the assurance of regular learning opportunities. It needs to be about '*holding onto the momentum, and holding onto the systems change commitment*'. This is not easy – it requires sharp, collaborative thinking and adaptive leadership that is comfortable and effective in an environment that is full of ambiguity and demands agility of thought and action. Above all, it relies on trust.

References

ACARA (2013), *National Report on Schooling in Australia 2013; Part 9, Additional Statistics*, http://docs.acara.edu.au/resources/ANR_2013_Part_9.pdf. [85]

Australian Bureau of Statistics (2016), *4221.0 - Schools, Australia, 2015*, http://www.abs.gov.au/AUSSTATS/abs@.nsf/DetailsPage/4221.02015?OpenDocument (accessed on 23 May 2018). [86]

Australian Bureau of Statistics (2016), *6227.0 - Education and Work, Australia, May 2015*, http://www.abs.gov.au/AUSSTATS/abs@.nsf/Previousproducts/6227.0Main Features1May 2015?opendocument&tabname=Summary&prodno=6227.0&issue=May 2015&num=&view= (accessed on 23 May 2018). [87]

Beacon Foundation (2018), *Beacon Foundation: eBeacon*, https://ebeacon.net.au/ebeacon/ (accessed on 25 May 2018). [94]

Beacon Foundation (2018), *Beacon Foundation: Real Futures Generation*, http://beaconfoundation.com.au/wp-content/uploads/2015/05/DL-Flyer-Master-Beacon-Web.pdf (accessed on 25 May 2018). [93]

Bruce, M. and J. Bridgeland (2014), *The Mentoring Effect: Young People's Perspectives on the Outcomes and Availability of Mentoring*, https://files.eric.ed.gov/fulltext/ED558065.pdf (accessed on 23 May 2018). [95]

Collaboration for Impact (2017), *Collaborative Change Cycle*, https://www.collaborationforimpact.com/collaborative-change-cycle/. [92]

Eslake, S. (2016), *Tasmania Report 2016*, http://www.tcci.com.au/getattachment/Events/Tasmania-Report-2016/Tasmania-Report-2016-FINAL.pdf.aspx. [83]

Parliament of Tasmania (2017), *2017-18-BP1-2-Tasmanian-Economy*. [84]

Parliament of Tasmania (2016), *Education Bill 2016*, Parliament of Tasmania, http://www.parliament.tas.gov.au/bills/Bills2016/reprint/55_of_2016.pdf (accessed on 23 May 2018). [88]

Tasmanian Government Department of Education (2018), *MyEducation*, https://my.education.tas.gov.au/Pages/default.aspx (accessed on 23 May 2018). [91]

Tasmanian Government Department of Education (2018), *Years 11 and 12*, https://11and12.education.tas.gov.au/ (accessed on 24 May 2018). [90]

Tasmanian Government Department of Education (2017), *Department of Education Annual Report*, https://documentcentre.education.tas.gov.au/Documents/DoE-Annual-Report-2016-17.pdf (accessed on 23 May 2018). [89]

ORGANISATION FOR ECONOMIC CO-OPERATION AND DEVELOPMENT

The OECD is a unique forum where governments work together to address the economic, social and environmental challenges of globalisation. The OECD is also at the forefront of efforts to understand and to help governments respond to new developments and concerns, such as corporate governance, the information economy and the challenges of an ageing population. The Organisation provides a setting where governments can compare policy experiences, seek answers to common problems, identify good practice and work to co-ordinate domestic and international policies.

The OECD member countries are: Australia, Austria, Belgium, Canada, Chile, the Czech Republic, Denmark, Estonia, Finland, France, Germany, Greece, Hungary, Iceland, Ireland, Israel, Italy, Japan, Korea, Latvia, Lithuania, Luxembourg, Mexico, the Netherlands, New Zealand, Norway, Poland, Portugal, the Slovak Republic, Slovenia, Spain, Sweden, Switzerland, Turkey, the United Kingdom and the United States. The European Union takes part in the work of the OECD.

OECD Publishing disseminates widely the results of the Organisation's statistics gathering and research on economic, social and environmental issues, as well as the conventions, guidelines and standards agreed by its members.

OECD PUBLISHING, 2, rue André-Pascal, 75775 PARIS CEDEX 16
(84 2018 03 1 P) ISBN 978-92-64-30487-1 – 2019

www.ingramcontent.com/pod-product-compliance
Ingram Content Group UK Ltd.
Pitfield, Milton Keynes, MK11 3LW, UK
UKHW051241300926
15471UKWH00015B/1447

9 789264 304871